KV-187-206

CHANGING CULTURES

The Nyamwezi Today

CHANGING CULTURES
General Editor: Jack Goody

The aim of this series is to show how specific societies and cultures, including sub-groups within more complex societies, have developed and changed in response to conditions in the modern world. Each volume will draw on recent fieldwork to present a comprehensive analysis of a particular group, cast in a dynamic perspective that relates the present both to the past of the group and to the external forces that have impinged upon it. The range of volumes in the series reflects the developing interests and concerns of the social sciences, especially social anthropology and sociology.

The Nyamwezi Today

A Tanzanian People in the 1970s

R.G. ABRAHAMS

*Lecturer in Social Anthropology, University of Cambridge
and Fellow of Churchill College, Cambridge*

CAMBRIDGE UNIVERSITY PRESS

CAMBRIDGE

LONDON   NEW YORK   NEW ROCHELLE
MELBOURNE   SYDNEY

Published by the Press Syndicate of the University of Cambridge
The Pitt Building, Trumpington Street, Cambridge CB2 1RP
32 East 57th Street, New York, NY 10022, USA
296 Beaconsfield Parade, Middle Park, Melbourne 3206, Australia

© Cambridge University Press 1981

First published 1981

Photoset, printed and bound
in Great Britain by
REDWOOD BURN LIMITED
Trowbridge & Esher

British Library Cataloguing in Publication Data
Abrahams, Raphael Garvin
The Nyamwezi today. – (Changing cultures).
1. Nyamwezi
I. Title   II. Series
301.29′678′28   DT443   80–41012
ISBN 0 521 22694 5 hard covers
ISBN 0 521 29619 6 paperback

Contents

Illustrations and tables

Preface

I first visited the Nyamwezi of west-central Tanzania in late 1957 as a Junior Research Fellow of the East African Institute of Social Research, and I lived among them and their fellow villagers for a little over two years collecting material for my doctorate and, as a friend there put it, 'growing up'. During the years which followed, my connection with and interest in them was maintained through academic work and a spasmodic correspondence; and it was with great pleasure and excitement – not untinged with diffidence about how welcome I might be after so long an interval – that I returned among them in 1974 for a further period of research and, with it, the opportunity to renew old ties and perhaps establish new ones. As was not surprising, a great deal that I had left behind was much the same. Many of the people I had known were still in the same area, though others had of course moved elsewhere or had died and yet others had grown from small children I had teased and played with into married men and women. Most people were still farmers trying to make a living out of their relatively unpromising soils, and much of their familial and religious life did not seem to be radically different. And to cap all this, the warmth and generosity of the hospitality which my former neighbours extended to me, and the testimony it gave that Nyamwezi society was still one of the most friendly and open that one could hope to encounter, made it tempting to feel that little had changed apart perhaps from oneself. For as an old acquaintance asked me as he surveyed my greying hairs, 'How can you have got so old while we are just the same?'

And yet, even my first journey in October 1974 from Kahama District Headquarters to Busangi, where I wished to stay again, brought evidence of serious change. The movement for political independence which I had witnessed at the local level in the late fifties had, of course, culminated not long after in the founding of the new state of Tanzania; and although the District Office was still housed in the same buildings as before, it was a Tanzanian Area Commissioner who now had given me permission to proceed out to the village where I was to live. The route I took carried me past the site of Butumwa village, where I had stayed on first arrival in the area and again for several months before I left in early 1960. The mud-brick house which my neighbours had built for me as a kindness and a token of their acceptance of me had almost disappeared – it had been used by others for a time and then gradually fallen into decay – but this was only the most personal part of a broader scene of desolation which Butumwa presented. Many of its houses and homesteads still stood, but the population had been moved with those of several other villages some weeks before to a site about a mile away which had been chosen by the government for a new large compact village settlement. Only one house within sight of where I stood was still occupied – by a young man and his wife who had been expecting a baby at the time of the move. They had been allowed to stay in their existing house for the time being. Most other villagers had gone to their plots in the new village where I found them in the often rather makeshift housing which they had hastily built for themselves until the opportunity arose to build more solid and elaborate accommodation. This new village was part of a national scheme to resettle the population of the country in large compact settlements which could, it was hoped, be better provided with schools and dispensaries and, eventually, even running water. It was also envisaged that the new communities would be able to engage in more productive forms of agriculture than the previous patterns of settlement permitted. In addition, although the point was played down somewhat at the time, it was assumed by many that the new 'development villages' (*vijiji vya maendeleo*), as they were called, would be encouraged to engage in *ujamaa* (socialist collective) enterprises. This and much else was as yet uncertain, but one thing at least was clear. Although change in itself was nothing new to Unyamwezi, never before had the Government and the state penetrated with such force and vigour into the inner recesses of village and domestic life.

There was further evidence of major change when I proceeded from this village to the nearby local government headquarters. The buildings were again much as I had left them, but they were no longer occupied by a local chief and his henchmen. I knew that chiefship as political office had been abolished several years before, and I now encountered for the first time the officers who replaced the chiefly regime. The former chief's house was now assigned to the Divisional Secretary, a TANU official and former teacher, and other houses were occupied by a magistrate and by another party man, the Ward Secretary. None of these was a local man and only the Ward Secretary spoke Nyamwezi. They conducted their official business in Swahili – Tanzania's national language – and it was clear that the area was being drawn more fully than ever before into the nation as a whole. Coupled with this, even young children, who now compulsorily attended primary school, were much more fluent in Swahili than when I had left, as I discovered for myself on the first day of my revisit. A young boy stood in front of me and in impeccable Swahili told me that his grandfather, an old friend, wanted to see me whom he also flatteringly called his grandfather.

It is some of these developments, continuities and changes that I try to document in the main body of this book; and I do so in the hope that I can present not simply a more up-to-date account of the 'condition' of the people, but also one which will do justice to some of the things that matter to them as they go about their lives in their new nation. In saying this I am aware that my account is a selective and a partial one, especially in its tendency to concentrate on major social structural features and developments. This is not to deny the significance of such phenomena as religious and other customary beliefs and practices either in their own right or in the roles they play *vis-à-vis* social structure, and I do in fact discuss such practices and roles at various junctures in this book. But my emphasis is on social structure, and while this no doubt reflects something of myself it also, I believe, reflects some real features of the Nyamwezi situation. Firstly, it is not hard to see that social structure has been the most immediate focus of large-scale planned change in the area. Secondly, as my comments about the open and hospitable nature of Nyamwezi society to some extent imply, it can be argued that the people of the area are themselves in many ways more interested in social relationships than in culture as such for its own sake. Customs, values and ideas tend to be of special interest to them when they are seen to possess a direct relevance to their relationships with each other and the outside world. Living well together is of prime importance to them, and the fact that people of often quite diverse origins typically achieve this in the villages of the area, without stress on uniformity in all fields of custom, is no mean testimony to their will and skill in this regard. Again, in external relations, as I argue in my final chapter, it is not so much the details of local custom that matter – they are changing all the time – but its possession as a kind of resource which gives local people a legitimate and dignified identity in their dealings with the wider powers that be.

These considerations lead on to a further complex issue. A first glance at the title of this book might suggest (quite wrongly I hope) that it is just another 'tribal study', with all the faults of that rather old-fashioned genre. The concept of 'tribe' and the nature of such studies have been subjected to severe criticism by both anthropologists and others (cf. Southall, 1970) on a variety of grounds. 'Tribe' itself, for instance, has been said with much justification to be a term which has been used more readily of modern Africans than modern Europeans without proper thought to the comparability of 'regional particular-ism' in the two continents.[1] This point can be dealt with fairly easily by dropping the offending word and using terms like 'ethnic group' or, more simply, 'people'; and I have tried to do this in this book wherever possible. But the problem is not simply one of choice of words. The idea of 'tribal study', however it is titled, has been attacked on at least equally serious grounds as both politically divisive and epistemologically unsound, inasmuch as it tends to over-emphasise and rigidify a fundamentally fluid and contextually very variable phenomenon. Leaving aside the wilder forms such arguments have taken, it is of course patently true that ethnicity is a shifting and a delicate phenomenon, often – though by no means always – with important political implications; and it is no accident, for example, that the Tanzanian government decided not to ask any questions about ethnic group membership in its 1978 National Census. On the other hand it is equally clear that such groups and categories are far from wholly insubstantial and avoidance of due reference to them would appear to be mistaken also. My approach in the present work is basically to recognise but not exaggerate the fact that there are Nyamwezi Tanzanians, about whom I am moderately well informed, and to try to write about them and the area they mostly live in as sensibly and sensitively as I can. Here, and in my previously published work (cf.1965, 1967a and b, 1970), I have paid a great deal of attention to the fact that Unyamwezi (Nyamwezi country) is not simply the area where Nyamwezi live, since many other people live there and share their lives with them, and many Nyamwezi live elsewhere. I have also tried to make it very clear that ethnic identity as such is rarely of great concern to them, compared for instance with living well together in local communities, and that they and their fellow villagers are very much aware how much they have in common with each other and how much their fates are intertwined in dealing with the outside world. In addition I have pointed out that neither the people nor their country constitute units with clearcut and unchanging boundaries. In working on this book I have been keenly conscious of the tension between trying to write simply and clearly and trying to do reasonable justice to the complex nature of such matters. I can only hope that I have not veered too far from either of these aims in the pursuit of the other.

Acknowledgements

Although the contents of this book are, of course, my own responsibility, it would not have been possible to collect and collate the material for it without a great deal of help from others both within and outside Unyamwezi. My 1974–5 visit to the area was financed by the Social Science Research Council and a grant from the University of Cambridge, who also helped with travel within Tanzania on my brief trip in December 1978. This last formed part of a wider visit to Tanzania arranged and funded by the University of Dar es Salaam and the Inter-University Council for Higher Education Overseas. I am extremely grateful for all this generous help, and also for the loan on moderate terms in 1974–5 of a Land-Rover and camping equipment by Professor Michael Day of St Thomas's Hospital, London. In addition, I would like to thank Dr Richard Leakey of the National Museum of Kenya and Miss L. Williams for help in sorting out the details of this latter loan. Similarly, I would like to thank Mr Derek Bryceson, Dr Abdulla Bujra, Mr Bill Gibbons, 'Mischa', Professor Cuthbert Omari, and the many other Tanzanian academics and officials who helped me to get these research trips off the ground. I am also grateful to the International African Institute for their permission to use part of my 1977 paper on 'Time and Village Structure' in Chapter 3.

An anthropologist is especially dependent on the hospitality and co-operation of others during fieldwork. In this context I would especially like to thank my friends Julius Brush of Kahama, Nsabila Kitambi of Kakola, Professor and Mrs Ian Livingstone, Peter and Zebiya Rigby, Dr and Mrs Diekema, and the many villagers and others in Unyamwezi who received me back again, or for the first time, with the heart-warming hospitality for which the area is renowned. They are too many for me to name them all but I would particularly like to mention Ibuli, Hansini, Lukuliko, Mayebele, Mayige, Misana, Mtambuko, Muyeye, Ndulichimu and his wife Kamunde (who cooked regularly for me) and their many neighbours in Busangi, who had been my friends and mentors in 1957–60 and welcomed me back 'home' again in 1974. I would also like to thank the villagers of Wame

and Kisuke for the generous hospitality they extended to me. Last
within Tanzania, but in no sense least, I wish to take this opportunity
to thank my friend and field assistant B. K. Kalugula for his invaluable
help and the great pleasure of his company during my two lengthier
stays in the area.

I am indebted to Mrs S. Hicks, Mrs S. Hogg, Mrs S. Polyviou, Mrs
D. Quarrie and Mrs K. Stringer for help at various stages in the preparation of the manuscript, and to Mr C. Lwoga, Mr E. Lukwaro, Mr S.
Rugumisa and a variety of colleagues for useful discussions and comments during the course of writing it. I am particularly grateful to Professor M. Fortes for valuable discussion of the data used in Chapters 3
and 4 and also to Professor J. Barnes and Professor J. Goody for
helpful comments at different stages in the preparation of my Chapter
4 material.

My wife Eeva and my children have put up with a great deal to make
this book possible, and I dedicate it to them in the hope that it is not too
unworthy of the patience and forbearance they have shown.

Map of Nyamwezi area

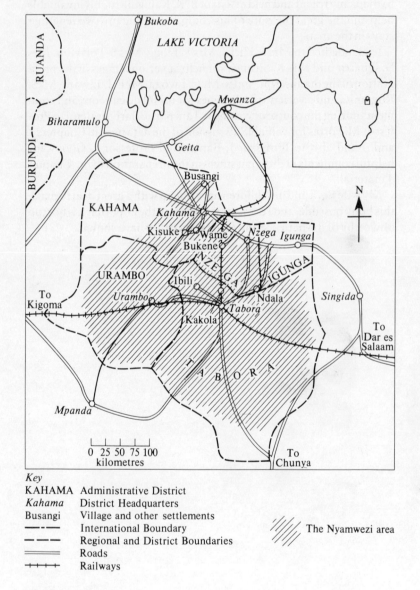

Key

KAHAMA	Administrative District
Kahama	District Headquarters
Busangi	Village and other settlements
—·—·	International Boundary
— — —	Regional and District Boundaries
═══	Roads
+++++	Railways

The Nyamwezi area

1 The people and their country

The Nyamwezi are a Tanzanian people. As is well known Tanzania consists of the mainland area formerly called Tanganyika and the off-shore islands of Zanzibar and Pemba which combined with the mainland to form the present United Republic of Tanzania in 1964. Its northern neighbours are Uganda (with whom it recently has been at war) and also Kenya, while to the west it borders on Ruanda, Burundi and Zaire. To the south are Zambia, Malawi and Mozambique. The country has an area (c. 940,000 square kilometres) some seven times the size of that of the United Kingdom, and a population of just over 17½ million according to the official 1978 census figures which were released to the Press in January 1979.

The Tanzanian mainland contains a wide variety of ecological zones including highland areas in the north and south, a coastal plain edged by the Indian ocean, and some very fertile lake-shore regions e.g. on the western side of Lake Victoria. There is also a large central tableland, which is sometimes called the 'cultivation steppe' and which includes the Nyamwezi area. This tableland is divided from the coast by the Masai plains and other relatively arid areas. The country has a number of important towns such as Dar es Salaam and Dodoma (the present and planned future capitals respectively), Arusha, Mwanza and Tabora, but the urban population is relatively small and over 90 per cent of Tanzanians live and farm in rural areas. As one might expect, the forms of farming they adopt – subsistence farming plus cash-cropping, for example, or pastoralism – vary considerably from one zone to another.

Although they are still culturally rather mixed and speak a wide variety of local languages, Tanzanians are of course politically, economically, and in other ways united within their nation whose official language, Swahili, is becoming increasingly well understood and widely used. Mainland Tanganyika became independent in December 1961 with the Tanganyika African National Union (TANU) as its widely supported ruling party. It formally became a one-Party state in 1965, though this did little more than bring the constitution into line with political reality. Since Independence the country has enjoyed the leadership and guidance of its regularly re-elected President, Julius Nyerere, who headed the Independence movement and is often fondly

1

spoken of by Tanzanians and others as '*Mwalimu*' (the teacher). In 1977 TANU was amalgamated with the ruling Afro-Shirazi Party of Zanzibar to form the new Revolutionary Party (*Chama cha Mapinduzi* or CCM). This, like TANU, is under President Nyerere's chairmanship and it has maintained TANU's commitment to socialist political and economic development and with it the avoidance of serious cleavages of wealth and power between different sections of the people. How well this is being achieved, and how best it might be so, has been the subject of considerable debate at various times within the country, and indeed outside, but the aim itself persists and appears genuinely to have helped to limit inequalities. The President himself has been the most important single architect of Tanzanian socialism, and his speeches and writings on the subject – the Arusha Declaration of 1967 for example, and his formulations of the related ideas of 'African socialism' and *Ujamaa* – have become internationally well known. For him, as Nellis (1972, p.102) has noted, 'economic affluence is inseparable from social justice', and Nyerere himself has written in his *Socialism and Rural Development* that the objective of socialism in Tanzania is

To build a society in which all members have equal rights and equal opportunities; in which all can live at peace ... without suffering or imposing injustice, being exploited or exploiting; and in which all have a gradually increasing basic level of material welfare before any individual lives in luxury. (Nyerere, 1967a, p.4)

It may be noted that the Swahili title of the above quoted work is *Ujamaa Vijijini* (literally socialism in the villages) and, as this suggests, a main element in the President's programme for socialist development has been an attempt to persuade the people to establish *ujamaa* (socialist collective) villages as the basic units of Tanzanian society. As will be seen, part of the present work (see especially Chapter 3) is devoted to examining the relevance of this for the Nyamwezi.

Being Tanzanians is important for the Nyamwezi, but this does not of course tell us much about which Tanzanians in particular they are. Nor is there any satisfactory single answer to this question. The first literary record of people called Nyamwezi appears to have been made by Europeans who visited the East African coast at the beginning of the nineteenth century, and the name itself seems to have developed out of trading contacts between inland peoples and coastal dwellers.

2

It probably at first meant simply 'westerners', and in the nineteenth century it seems to have been used at least occasionally to describe both those who came from what is commonly known today as *Unyamwezi* (Nyamwezi country) and some of their neighbours to the west and north. Such directional names have been fairly common in this region as elsewhere in the world. Thus the closely related people living to the north of Unyamwezi bear the name Sukuma, which is vernacular for 'north', and this term is also used more generally in the area to refer (with a small 's' as it were) to any people including Nyamwezi who are living to one's north.

The relativity of such names suggests that the Nyamwezi might perhaps be best considered as those who simply happen to be or to have been called such by others. There is an element of truth in this, but the situation is in fact more complex. For although there can be argument about the long-term stability, exact location, and blurred nature of some of its boundaries, the people's home area of west-central Tanzania has come to be widely known as Unyamwezi both by themselves and by others and the name has nowadays lost its former directional connotations. In addition, there is a Bantu language (*Kinyamwezi*), whose edges are again not wholly clearcut, and a range of local custom, albeit varied, changing and not always followed, which are considered to be Nyamwezi; and at least as importantly, there are a large number of people – probably well over half a million of them these days – who are likely in some contexts to describe themselves as Nyamwezi alongside of, and indeed as part of, being Tanzanians. The contexts in question vary from official ones, of court procedures, for example, and census returns at least up to 1967, to a wide range of more informal situations in which people wish to make a broad comparison between themselves and others. Like the origin of the name itself, some of these situations arise from travel to towns and rural areas outside Unyamwezi. People on such occasions may seek help from other Nyamwezi, or they may engage in forms of institutionalised joking, *utani*, which are customary between them and the members of some comparable groups near the coast such as the Zaramu and Zigua peoples, and they may also seek help from these joking partners. On other occasions, the term may be used within Unyamwezi itself, perhaps to differentiate the people from some immigrant groups such as the Tusi, who come from areas like Kigoma Region and Burundi to the west and north-west, or more generally to draw attention to some quality of character or an area of custom which they attribute to themselves, sometimes in self-praise or self-criticism, as a mark of their identity. I discuss the relevance of custom for the people in some detail later (see especially Chapter 5). As to qualities of character, it is of course notoriously difficult to generalise without drifting into caricature on issues of this sort. It may perhaps be mentioned here, however, that many Nyamwezi see themselves quite justifiably as a very sociable and hospitable people in their dealing with their fellow villagers and with others to whom they feel they can relate on friendly and roughly equal terms; and they also know that they may at times seem to be unreliable to those who try to get them to agree to do things which they are not very keen to do. For they often prefer to appear to accede to a request and then fail for some reason to fulfil it, rather than to refuse outright and perhaps give offence; and they base this on a liking for politeness coupled with a not unreasonable premiss that people should be very sensitive about what they try to demand of others.

All this goes with great care in their use of words more generally, and with an emphasis also upon proper etiquette which is most immediately clear in their customary greetings to each other when they meet. No encounter is normally allowed to become a 'business' one until the persons concerned have enquired, often at some length, about each other's health and the state of their homes and families, and even then the main matter to be dealt with may often be approached gradually and indirectly rather than 'full-frontally'. Such behaviour can easily appear pedantic to a less formally-minded outsider, and I myself initially found it frustrating on occasion, but it is valued locally for the contribution which it makes to orderly and productive relationships between parties who are seen to demonstrate a mutual respect and voice a mutual concern for each other. These qualities of sensitivity and concern are, I may add, also clearly visible in the local patterns of hospitality. A respected and not simply casual visitor is not merely generously fed. Careful efforts are made to ensure that he retains his own identity during a visit and does not simply become his host's dependant. He should ideally be provided with his own place to stay which will serve as his own base of social operations, and food and drink should be provided both for his consumption and disposal. On one visit on which I accompanied a friend, beer was brought for us in a hut set aside for our visit, and this was ours and ours alone to drink and distribute to others who then became our guests. Again, in 1974–5 arrangements were made for the wife and daughter-

4

in-law of an old friend who lived nearby to cook for me during my stay. I was told that I could not pay for these services directly but if I wished to help out with the family's needs from time to time, that was up to me and would be welcome. Food was brought the fifty yards or so to my tent each day and enough was always brought for me to be able to share with at least one other person comfortably. I was always genuinely welcome to drop in and share food with the family but the arrangements were designed to ensure that I could be both host and guest.

Most Nyamwezi speak Kinyamwezi as their mother tongue and either live in or come from the Nyamwezi area. In addition to this, however, there is a widespread notion that ethnic identity – being Nyamwezi or Sumbwa or Tusi for example – is inherited from one's father. Thus it is possible for a young man born in Dar es Salaam and growing up speaking mainly Swahili to classify himself as Nyamwezi on this basis, and it is similarly possible for long-term residents of Unyamwezi to hark back to their own father's non-Nyamwezi origins. On the other hand, it is also true that such latter persons and their descendants can fairly easily begin to characterise themselves as Nyamwezi if they wish to do so, and I have met people who have 'become' Nyamwezi in this way, and may describe themselves as having done so, after being born in the country, or coming as a child, and residing there for many years. That such change is possible is in keeping with the open nature of Nyamwezi society. So too, however, is the further important fact that, with the partial exception of Tusi immigrants from the west and north-west, ethnic identity is not normally of great practical significance in the internal social system of the area's local communities; and it appears that these days even the Tusi have started to become more fully absorbed into the fabric of rural society despite their deep interest in pastoralism, a tendency to emphasise their own cultural distinctiveness, and an earlier common preference, associated with both these features, for keeping themselves residentially apart from others and marrying among themselves (cf. Abrahams, 1970).

Historically, an important factor in this situation of fluidity and openness, and at the same time a main source of continuity and order, was the institution of Nyamwezi chiefship (*butemi*). This, like the system which replaced it after Independence, provided a territorial frame – or rather a series of such frames, since the area was never unified politically under a single chief – within which people could move fairly easily from one place to another. Each chiefdom had a ruling family whose ancestors are usually said to have come into the area many generations ago. The country is typically described as having been empty or, at most, only sparsely populated at that time, and the newcomers are said to have carved out domains for themselves which at first expanded and then subdivided as the population grew. Sometimes they are said to have usurped the power of a previously established group. New subjects, both from other Nyamwezi chiefdoms and beyond, appear generally to have been welcomed by the chiefs and their subordinate authorities who gave them land and offered them political and ritual security in return for orderly behaviour, tribute and allegiance. Provided these were given without hindrance, little if any direct pressure seems to have been put on non-Nyamwezi by a chief or his subordinates to change their ethnic identity or special patterns of behaviour in such areas as marriage, religious ritual and food taboos. A similarly undemanding pattern was found also at the village level where a main concern, as I have already noted, has been that all villages should co-operate and live well together rather than all slavishly follow the same customs as a matter of principle. It is clear, however, that Unyamwezi's chiefdoms and villages have served nonetheless as a kind of melting pot in which a substantial degree of customary uniformity has tended to emerge in this atmosphere of tolerance as a natural development from the interactions of their members. It may also be mentioned in this context that, despite their own external provenance, the ruling families have in many ways been perceived as Nyamwezi *par exellence*. By virtue of their royal birth and office, chiefs were held to be the ritual and political 'owners' of their chiefdom and it was in considerable part through attachment to them as kin and/or subjects that the connection between many Nyamwezi and their country, Unyamwezi, was traditionally established and maintained.

I have dwelt at some length on these questions of identity because it seems important to affirm that fluidity, change and contextual variation – in short '*becoming*' – are as much a feature of the situation as are persistence or stability and '*being*'. The latter qualities are undoubtedly of great significance but they are usually more easily grasped and expressed, and they tend to be all the more deceptive for this. In the present case they can all too easily obscure both the normality of change and the fact that openness, both to new people and to new ideas, has been a major feature of the vitality which I believe characterises Nyamwezi society and culture.

The Nyamwezi area today is about 90,000 square kilometres in extent and it covers most of the Tabora, Urambo, Nzega and Igunga Districts of Tanzania's Tabora Region and the neighbouring eastern half of Kahama District in Shinyanga Region. It is part of the Tanzanian 'cultivation steppe', and it mostly consists of undulating country about 1,200 metres above sea level. There are some rocky hills and ridges rising as much as 300 metres above the general level of the country, and lower though occasionally spectacular outcrops of bare granite rock are fairly common. There are some rivers but they do not usually flow during the drier months. The year falls into two main divisions, a rainy season when the people are most actively engaged in agriculture, and a dry season when there is more suitable opportunity for travel, housebuilding and leisure. The main period of rainfall is between November and April. Precipitation averages around 85 centimetres per year but it is rather variable from year to year and place to place, and it is by no means always well distributed within a single rainy season. Mean average temperatures in the area are around 23 degrees centigrade and they range between mean maxima of about 29 degrees to mean minima of about 17 degrees.

In most parts of the country a regular sequence of vegetation zones is found. Lower levels of grass or thorn bush acacia steppe, known locally as *mbuga*, are succeeded by higher levels of park steppe and woodland including some thick forest. *Mbuga* areas are often liable to flood in the wet season and they are as such largely uninhabited, though they are used for pasture and some agriculture. Some forest areas, on the other hand, yield little or no ground water and this, coupled with their poor soils in many cases and their abundance of insect pests, including tsetse, can make them relatively unattractive for settlement. In general, the most settled areas are those of park steppe and relatively well-watered woodland, though even here the soils are often not especially good.

Despite the regularity of these patterns, too static a view of the topography of the region needs to be avoided. The overall appearance of the country in the rainy season is quite different from that in the drier months when dull clouds and lush greenery give way to bright skies, dry dust and sear vegetation; and the opening up of an area to settlement of course sharply affects its character over time. Tracts of almost treeless country may be found which once were woodland and have since been cleared, and secondary bush quickly springs up in areas where settlement has been abandoned. Such processes of transformation still go on today and parts of the area have changed radically in the last thirty years as they have been subject to intensive settlement by newcomers from other parts of Unyamwezi or nearby. The Igunga area to the east of Nzega is a major case in point. In the early 1940s it was a remote and fairly sparsely populated part of Nzega District, and it began about that time to attract increasing numbers of Sukuma settlers, often with large herds of cattle, from Shinyanga District to the north. Some cotton cash-cropping began to develop there in the 1950s when a local ginnery was opened as an experiment. By the 1970s the area was much more accessible since a major east–west trunk road now passed through it, and big cattle-owners were beginning to be pushed south into Tabora District and beyond as the population increased and more and more land was taken up for cotton and food crops.[1] Igunga is nowadays a well-connected, prosperous and relatively densely settled part of the country and it recently became an Administrative District in its own right. It may also be mentioned here that some parts of southern Kahama District, such as Mpunze and Ushetu, have experienced large influxes of human and cattle population in more recent years, and here, as elsewhere in the past, tsetse fly appears to have been driven back as settlement has rapidly expanded.

Agriculture supplemented by animal husbandry is the mainstay of Nyamwezi economic life. Mostly it is carried out on family fields with family labour supplemented at key times by neighbours, relatives and some hired help, but there have been some communal ventures in *ujamaa* villages (see Chapter 3). Most cultivation is still done by hand-hoe, but the use of ox-ploughs has increased and tractors are beginning to be used for work in some *mbuga* areas and other suitable terrain. The use of tractors, however, is of course very much dependent upon internationally determined fuel costs and supplies and seems unlikely to increase dramatically in the near future. A wide variety of crops are grown, though not all of them are equally popular and viable in all parts of the area and some noticeable changes have occurred in preferences over the last twenty years. Bulrush millet, for example, was a major crop in northern Unyamwezi in the 1950s, but it was much less widely grown in 1974–5. This appears to have been due to a complex combination of mainly technical factors, including a shift of preference towards maize as a relatively high yield crop, and also increasing difficulties in coping with birds which have always been a nuisance but which became more and more devastating as they concentrated on a diminishing millet acreage. One reason for the increased preference for maize has been the need for more land and more time for cash crops, especially cotton and tobacco which are now much more extensively grown in the area than was the case at the close of the colonial period. People are aware, however, that maize takes more out of the soil and is a less drought-resistant crop than either bulrush millet or sorghum, which has apparently also become less popular than it used to be, and there is some evidence that the trend away from these two crops may have been reversed a little in more recent years.

Rice is another cash crop of importance and some sunflower is also grown for sale. Rice also appears to be eaten more often than it was in the 1950s. The main staple food, however, remains stiff porridge (*bugalli*), made with flour from maize or other grain (or on occasion from cassava), and it is eaten either with meat or, more commonly, with a vegetable relish made perhaps from beans, or mushrooms, or leaves of spinach or cassava, and commonly cooked in a groundnut base. Sweet potatoes are also grown – these are the traditional food, with groundnuts, for lunch breaks during agricultural work – and some people with access to good water supplies also produce onions and tomatoes and some tree-borne fruits including oranges. Bananas are grown in some places but they are mainly eaten as a fruit, rather than as a staple food as in some other areas of East Africa. Apart of course from water, the most common drink is local beer, made from maize or sorghum, and this is especially popular at weekends. Some distilled alcohol and also tea, coffee and soft drinks are also occasionally consumed.

The most important livestock holdings are in cattle, of which there are close upon 1½ million in the area. The numbers held in any one place tend to vary with the incidence of population movement and they have risen greatly in many districts owing to the immigration of large numbers of Sukuma, often with big herds. Tusi immigration was important in the past in this respect but is much less so today. Disease can seriously reduce cattle numbers, and it is not always easily controlled. In the past rinderpest and east-coast fever took widespread toll of cattle holdings, but the main problems I have recently observed appear to be confined to particular localities. For instance many cattle were dying in and immediately around Busangi village in the early 1970s, while they appeared to be flourishing in other parts of the wider area administered from there. In addition to cattle, smallstock in the form of goats and sheep and also chickens are kept by the people.

Wildlife is also a source of meat, but hunting is very strictly controlled these days after a relatively free period following Independence. Some hunts are carried out with nets, and individual hunters also pursue game with rifles, modern shot guns or old fashioned muzzle-loading, smooth-bore weapons. Some parts of Unyamwezi previously well stocked with game have become depleted of it, not so much because of hunting as because of human population movement into them. This is true of parts of the Igunga area, for example, and also of some parts of northern Kahama District. It may be noted here that hunting has a long and important history in Unyamwezi. The founders of ruling dynasties are typically said to have come originally as hunters into their eventual domains, and elephant hunting for ivory was a dangerous but very profitable activity in the nineteenth century. Moreover, although relatively few people have regularly engaged in hunting in recent decades it still has romantic appeal and is the masculine pursuit *par excellence* in the eyes of many Nyamwezi.

Although the people are dependent on their agriculture for survival, it is important to stress that theirs has not typically been a closed economy. As my earlier discussion of their name implied, the Nyamwezi had already started in the early nineteenth century to be well known for their long-distance trading journeys to the coast and elsewhere,[2] and their country subsequently began to be regularly visited by traders from the coast. These included Indian, Swahili, and Arab merchants and some of these founded the first settlement at Tabora which they initially called Kazé. Very many thousands of Nyamwezi travelled to the coast during the nineteenth century as traders or as porters on large caravans, and many have travelled widely during the present century as labour migrants to agricultural estates and elsewhere. Such labour migration, which was still quite popular in the 1950s, and the earlier participation in the caravan trade seem to have had their romantic and adventurous side, but they were nonetheless fundamentally responses to economic opportunities and pressures. Light soils and unpredictable rainfall tend in themselves to make agriculture somewhat precarious in this part of Tanzania, and it is not surprising that the people have been tempted to seek wealth from external sources. There has also been, however, a long and complex feedback to their agricultural activities from their involvement with the outside world. Nineteenth-century warfare and raiding between chiefdoms and the emergence of major warrior chiefs such as Mirambo, whom Stanley dubbed 'Napoleon of Central Africa', seem at least in part to have been the result of the increased commercial activity in the area and the attraction of the rewards which its control might offer; and they placed agricultural production under serious strain in many areas, as did demands for tax from subsequent colonial regimes. Labour migration itself, which was in part a response to these latter demands, tended to take manpower away from farming and thus to undermine further the agricultural base it was designed to supplement, though migrants do seem to have tried very hard to gain the maximum economic benefit from their work. It is interesting in this last respect that the main areas of Nyamwezi labour migration have shifted more than once – for example, from sisal estates to the clove plantations of Pemba and later to the cotton-growing districts of Sukumaland – as these became more or less preferable sources of income, both in terms of wages to be earned and, in the case of Sukumaland, the social and economic convenience of working there. In the years since Independence, migration for labour appears to have decreased significantly with the development of more successful forms of locally-based cash-crop production, though this in turn is not without its problems for subsistence agriculture as I have already briefly noted. It may be added that the consequent decrease in migration to more distant places has not inhibited population movement within Unyamwezi itself and on its outskirts, and indeed such movement has if anything increased as people have felt more pressed to seek better land on which to grow their wider range of cash and subsistence crops. It remains to be seen, as I discuss in Chapter 3, whether new forms of village organisation will seriously inhibit such mobility.

Up-to-date figures are not available on the numbers of people living outside Unyamwezi since, as I have noted, ethnic identity has tended to be played down in post-Independence censuses. However, just over a quarter of the Nyamwezi recorded in the 1957 census were listed as living outside the area and about half of these were living in immediately surrounding districts. Most of the remainder were recorded in the coastal region, and there is reason to believe that some of these would have designated themselves differently in their home territories. Some members of smaller neighbouring groups, such as the Konongo to the south-west, would call themselves Nyamwezi on the coast, where the Nyamwezi were better known and had a good reputation. Some Nyamwezi on the coast were permanently settled there while others were there merely temporarily for work. It is the numbers of this last group of short-term residents which are of course most likely to be affected by the development of cash crops in recent years. As such one might still expect to find a considerable proportion of the people (perhaps 15 to 20 per cent) living outside the main Nyamwezi area, though a majority of these would be settled in neighbouring rural areas. It should also be emphasised here that many of the people's neighbours are themselves quite mobile, and there are usually a number of non-Nyamwezi living in the villages of the area, as will be clear from my earlier discussion. The proportion of Nyamwezi in the villages commonly ranges from about 50 to 75 per cent,[3] and the identity of 'outsiders' varies, predictably enough, from one part of the country to another. Most of them speak Kinyamwezi at least reasonably well and many come from areas where the prevailing cultures are not in the main radically different. This is especially so in the case of their northern neighbours, the Sukuma, who are by far the biggest immigrant group, and it also holds to a considerable extent for their immediate western and north-western neighbours, the Sumbwa, who form the next largest contingent. As I have mentioned, Tusi pastoralists have, at least in the past, been the most poorly integrated immigrants. They appear to constitute a little under 5 per cent of the total population of the area.

It will be very clear already that Nyamwezi social and political institutions have been rather well adapted to absorbing newcomers including immigrants from other ethnic groups. Villages and the traditional and modern wider political units conjoining them have based their membership on well-developed incorporative principles of neighbourhood and territorial citizenship; and the more restrictive principle of birth and kinship has in general not been a key element in local grouping, though it is significant in other ways. The traditional ruling families of the area have of course constituted a partial exception to this last assertion, but their members have typically formed only a minority, albeit historically a very influential one, of the population of their 'home' territories and their subdivisions. I shall deal with these main fields of social structure in some detail in ensuing chapters. It may be noted here, however, that in addition to marriage ties between previously unrelated persons (for known kin should not marry), people are also linked here as elsewhere by interpersonal ties of friendship, which in the past took the form of blood-brotherhood, and there are various widespread ritual and other associations, including some whose origins lie outside Unyamwezi, which recruit members into local branches and play some part in achieving social integration in the area. Like marriage, both friendship and associations tend to cut across the boundaries of kinship linkage and even across those of ethnic groups, though the insularity of Tusi immigrants has been of relevance here, especially with regard to marriage and also, to a lesser degree, with regard to association membership. It is of interest in this context of the incorporation of diverse elements in the population that the ceremonies of initiation into some associations suggest strongly in their words and actions that the groups are in part a substitute for kinship among those who join them. Membership in associations is to a large extent voluntary, though people may feel constrained to join them on the advice of a diviner after suffering some illness or misfortune. Their activities are usually conducted at irregular intervals on an *ad hoc* basis when a need or suitable occasion arises. Most associations have their distinctive forms of dance, usually to drums. A few indeed are basically dance societies, but most of them are primarily concerned with ritual activities, though they also occasionally provide material help for their members in addition to giving them a more general sense of belonging to a group. Some, like the *Baswezi* and the *Bamigabo*, are especially concerned with spirit possession, some with divination, and others like the *Bayeye* and *Bagoyange* specialise in snake-charming and the cure of snakebite. There is even a society of porcupine hunters, *Banunguli*, and there are also other less esoteric hunting societies, such as the *Badandu*, which pursue more usual forms of game. The senior members of these latter groups typically combine great hunting skill with a locally much-admired knowledge of hunting medicines.

As references to the mobility of people in the area might suggest, communications are in fact quite well developed there and much used, though it is also true that such mobility long antedates the provision of modern road and rail facilities. The Central Railway from Dar es Salaam to Kigoma on Lake Tanganyika passes through Tabora and connects there with a line to Mwanza in the north which passes through Shinyanga and fairly close to both Nzega and Kahama. Main roads also link these urban centres with each other and the coast (via Nzega and Igunga), and there are also roads, albeit of varying quality, to outlying places. Buses normally run between main centres and from these to many rural areas at least once per day and sometimes more frequently than that, but services were curtailed temporarily in 1978–9 by the use of vehicles for troop movements in the war against

Uganda. Telecommunications and main postal services are largely restricted to the towns but letters can reach rural areas quite quickly. There is an airport at Tabora but air travel is almost wholly confined to expatriates, urban business men, and important officials, and services are not particularly frequent.

Although the local towns are still not especially large, their populations have been growing rapidly (Tabora's, the largest, had increased from about 12,000 in 1957 to over 67,000 in 1978) and they are the main administrative and commercial centres of the areas which surround them. They contain District and, in the case of Tabora and Shinyanga, Regional offices of Government Departments and of the ruling Revolutionary Party (CCM). Most towns also contain a branch of the National Bank of Commerce and a hospital. The banks are not much used as yet by rural Nyamwezi, but many villagers do come into town for consultation and hospital treatment if rural facilities, in the form of indigenous practitioners or local government dispensaries, are unable to handle their problems satisfactorily. The departure of many European staff during the years of Independence has to some extent coincided with a running-down of some larger Asian-owned shops in the main towns, though some survive, as do the lively urban markets. Some European-style foodstuffs, however, such as bread are in better supply than they used to be because of the development of a firm demand for them among the modern urban population, in addition to the continuing needs of missionaries and also of some expatriate technical experts who can still be found in Tabora and elsewhere. In general, and despite many connections between town and country, urban society and culture differs in a range of ways from that of villages, and people are clearly aware of this. Thus, there is a higher incidence of house-ownership by women in the towns, more renting of both rooms and houses, and a broader tendency for all transactions to become commercial. There is a greater ethnic mixture there – though Nyamwezi usually form the largest single element in urban populations – and an excess typically of males over females owing to the occupational structure which draws many men in from outside. Swahili is the main language used in urban centres, though this varies to some extent with speaker and context, and there are a number of 'sub-cultures' – of the bureaucratic elite, for example, or the often Muslim, longer-term inhabitants of towns – which are not well represented in most parts of the surrounding countryside.

14

In addition to town shops there are also smaller shops in many villages. In the 1950s most such shops were owned and run by Arabs, who are still found in considerable numbers in some places such as Mwanhala near Nzega, but the proportion under local African control has increased greatly since that time. Such shops usually stock a variety of goods including soap, paraffin, some patent medicines, blankets, cloth, some clothing, torch batteries, tea, cigarettes, matches, sweets, soft drinks and, occasionally, stationery. Meat is sold from time to time by part-time butchers. There has been a tendency in recent years for local co-operative organisations to take over the running of village shops, and certain goods like hoes and sugar tend in any case to be sold through official stores and other agencies. Supplies of goods are not always regular either in urban or in rural settlements. Shortages of such things as hoes, sugar, matches, beer and soft drinks have occurred quite often and have been a source of considerable dissatisfaction in both this and other parts of Tanzania.

It is often difficult to assess the wealth of individual villagers in the region. Although some families put on more elaborate weddings than others, conspicuous consumption is not particularly common, and people's reactions to enquiries about their money are no more positive than those of an average Englishman asked about his bank balance, though here as in other contexts they are more likely to prevaricate than to be rude. Nor is wealth in cattle always immediately obvious since large herds may be divided and not kept simply in one place; also, at least at first sight, some extremely rich cattle-owners could easily be mistaken, from their deceptively shabby clothes and unpretentious manner, for fairly poor men. In general, living standards seem to have improved since the late 1950s, though most villagers are still quite poor by northern European standards. Houses are still usually of mud-brick or mud and wattle construction with thatched roofs, but they more often have solidly made doors and unglazed wooden window frames with wooden shutters nowadays, and corrugated iron roofs, though not the general rule, also seem to be more common than they were. Bicycles are still a popular form of transport, though it is not clear that their numbers have greatly increased, and cars in private ownership are still rare. There are more radios than there used to be as a result of the 'transistor revolution'. People generally wear better clothes these days, and they also seem to buy more meat. Much more cash is available to them for these and other needs but prices have unfortunately moved quite steeply upwards in more recent years.

There are few signs as yet of a serious development of economic class divisions in the rural population in the last ten years. Most important in this context is the absence of a rural landless class. Some villagers are, however, considerably wealthier than others and, as Polly Hill (1972) has shown for the Hausa of northern Nigeria, even small differences can significantly assist one person to cope more successfully than another with seasonal shortages and other temporary economic difficulties. A few villagers are beginning to make money from hiring out ox-carts and also plough oxen, and some possess large holdings of one or two hundred cows and even many more than this,[4] whereas most cattle-owners tend to have rather smaller herds. Cattle are still considered to be both the most prestigious and, with good luck, the most profitable form of wealth, and people still contrast them, not unreasonably, with money which does not, they say, reproduce itself. Differences of wealth in cattle are, however, partly mitigated by the fact, which villagers are also well aware of, that the size of livestock holdings may easily rise or fall substantially through redistributive mechanisms, such as bridewealth or inheritance, and through local fluctuations in animal health and disease. Moreover, the fact that richer and poorer members of the rural population interact daily in a complex variety of ways, and to a large extent still have the same everyday life-style and domestic work patterns, tends to make differences between them rather less obvious to the people than those between villagers in general and some urban dwellers, including unfortunately even some of the salaried officials who are, paradoxically, committed to preventing the development of deeply entrenched inequalities in Tanzanian society.

A noteworthy development in Unyamwezi and in Tanzania generally since Independence has been the introduction of free compulsory primary education which began as early as 1964 in some parts of the country. The full effects of this will naturally enough not be seen for many years, but one immediately observable result is a substantial increase in the number of young people of both sexes who can speak Swahili. There was never much of a problem with this in the past in the case of Nyamwezi adult men whose travels for labour, or in earlier days for trade, provided them with both the need and opportunity to learn Swahili, though it may be noted that the recent shift away from labour migration and towards cash-cropping might well have tended eventually, had it had free play, to decrease the numbers of men fluent in the language. As late as the 1950s, however, children and women in the rural areas did not usually learn to speak it except in villages close to and influenced by Tabora town. In addition to their learning to speak Swahili nowadays, children are of course also learning to read and write it in the primary schools, and it is felt, not without reason, that literacy in the national language is a significant part of their education into Tanzanian citizenship. Civic education and what the President has called evocatively 'Education for self reliance' form a consciously important part of schooling in addition to the usual 'three Rs'. Children can be seen and heard first thing in the morning running round their village with their teachers and singing a variety of Tanzania's national songs in a systematic effort to combine physical fitness with political awareness; and agricultural or other 'self-reliance' training also forms an intrinsic element in the school curriculum. Such compulsory primary schooling is, however, not wholly without problems at the present time. Girls have traditionally played a substantial working role in domestic life from quite an early age and their help, like that of boys in herding smallstock and at special points in the agricultural season such as when birds need to be scared away from crops, cannot always easily be forgone. Because of difficulties of this sort, some parents keep their children out of school from time to time though they can be, and indeed sometimes are, prosecuted and fined for doing so. Another difficulty, which lies in the opposite direction, as it were, is that many parents would like their children to be able to continue their education beyond the primary school level. Places in higher-level schools are very scarce, however, and both Government and people were by no means wholly satisfied in 1974–5 with the working of the examination system which was being used to decide allocations. How well its replacement has worked is not yet clear. This was designed to place a greater weight on headmasters' assessments, but in 1975 people were not slow to point out that such an arrangement was itself possibly open to abuse.

It may be mentioned here that in addition to the educational arrangements for schoolchildren, there has also been an active adult literacy programme in the villages. Classes are held regularly and are taught by volunteers in an informal way and often in the open air. Such a programme is potentially important since large numbers of adults still could not properly read and write with any fluency at the time of my 1974–5 visit. How successful it will be in the longer term must depend very strongly not only on the quality of teaching and the

A street in Kahama Town, 1974–5 (note the contrast with the village below).

An adult literacy group in Busangi village in late 1974.

enthusiasm of the class members, but also on the extent to which there are genuine opportunities after a course has finished to keep up the skills acquired. It may be noted in this regard that a series of official publications, including booklets on Party policy, economic development, and the Party constitution, is available to people in the rural areas in addition to more local documentation of meetings and their decisions.

It remains to say a little in this chapter on the subject of religion, which I have so far only touched upon in passing and will not be dealing with in detail later. With the main exceptions of the rural areas around Tabora, where there are many largely Muslim villages, and of the areas around some Christian missions which have even produced high-ranking Nyamwezi church officials, neither Islam nor Christianity has taken an extensive hold in Unyamwezi's rural areas. The reasons for this situation are quite complex. The spread of Islam in the villages around Tabora appears to have owed a great deal to the influence of certain chiefs, such as Saidi Fundikira of Unyanyembe, rather than to direct interaction with the Arabs of the area, though more general urban contacts and travel to the Muslim coastal regions have also played their part. The acceptance of polygamy by Islam and the fact that there are no Muslim missionaries to exercise discipline over beer drinking, which in contrast to the coastal areas is popular in both Muslim and non-Muslim Nyamwezi villages, have further facilitated the acceptance of the religion.

Although some chiefs were Christians, Christianity did not receive much strong support from any really powerful Nyamwezi chief with influence over a wide area, and the presence of missionaries has, I suspect, been something of a hindrance to the spread of the religion at the same time as they have zealously tried to promote it. It was all too easy for a Christian mission in the past to appear to be competing for both land and 'subjects' with a chief, and indeed with the colonial government;[5] and the natural tendency of missionaries to try to keep a sharp eye on the Christian moral standards of the members of their congregations is also likely to have deterred quite a few potential converts. Certainly, Christian codes of conduct with regard to sexual relations, marriage, alcohol and participation in some forms of indigenous dance and ritual do not easily fit into the patterns of normal Nyamwezi village and domestic life. Moreover, it is important to remember in this context that the people have their own religious beliefs and practices which appear to have satisfied the needs

19

of most of them.

Nyamwezi religion, like Nyamwezi society itself, and unlike most forms of mission Christianity, is flexibly accretive rather than exclusive in its character. As one might expect in a religion without either 'church' or sects, there is little seeking in it for systemic unity, and there is also no attempt to insist that it forms a package which is equally significant for all. Indeed, the general tendency within it is for individuals, in an atmosphere of considerable tolerance, gradually to acquire their own constellation of belief and ritual and cult membership in the course of and through the interpretation of their life experience. It is not surprising in this light that an early Christian missionary was roundly told that all men know that God exists and that the various rules and prohibitions which he, the missionary, preached were best regarded as his own personal set of taboos.[6]

Beliefs in a high god are indeed widely held by Nyamwezi and a variety of terms are used to describe him such as *Likube* (identifying him as supreme being), *Limatunda* (identifying him as creator), *Limi* (identifying him as the sun), and *Liwelelo* (the universe). No special cult is addressed to the High God but he is customarily invoked before sacrifices to the ancestors.

Ancestor worship is the most important single element in the religious complex of the area. The ancestors of chiefs and their subordinate rulers are still held by many to affect the lives of those who live within their former territories, and their influence on rainfall has been particularly respected, but most spirits of the dead only affect their own descendants or, occasionally, those of their siblings. The spirits of dead twins are particularly thought able to affect living kinsfolk who are not descended from them.

Offerings to ancestors are made on a variety of occasions. Mostly they follow the advice of a diviner in response to a misfortune such as illness but some offerings are made regularly at points in the agricultural year, at planting and harvesting for instance, and they may also be given at events such as a birth or marriage, and when embarking on or returning safely from an important journey. The form of offering varies from libations of sorghum flour mixed with water (a mixture known as *lwanga*), through offerings of grain, beer or porridge to blood sacrifice usually of sheep and goats. The slaughter of cattle is normally reserved for sacrifices to royal ancestors. Most offerings take place at the homestead of the offerer – small shrines in the form of simple huts of grass and twigs some two to three feet high are set up there for the ancestor concerned – but, those to royal ancestors are also commonly made at their graves which are often marked by large old trees.

Offerings are usually made to male ancestors who may be either on the father's or the mother's side though paternal ancestors seem to be more commonly involved. Ancestors are generally considered to be well disposed to their descendants if the latter pay them due respect. It is believed, however, that an ancestor who feels neglected will bring misfortune, usually in the form of sickness, upon the negligent descendant or his children. Ancestors do not normally appear to punish offences between the living, though they may do so if they are invoked in indignation by one of their descendants, and it is mainly the failure to make proper offerings to them which they are said to resent.

A variety of non-ancestral spirits are also believed to influence the lives of men, and some of these, such as the *swezi* and *migabo* spirits, are the focus of the spirit possession societies and cults which individuals who have been attacked and possessed by them must join in order to obtain relief from their disturbing influence. Oaths and curses are also held to possess dangerous powers.

Beliefs in witchcraft and sorcery (*bulogi*) are also widespread in the area and sorcerers are considered to possess a range of techniques including spells and poisoning to attack their enemies. Sickness and death are the misfortunes most commonly attributed to them, but they are also said occasionally to attack crops and livestock. In 1974 I came across a case in the new village of Busangi where accusations of witchcraft arose against a man who had unwisely boasted – apparently in a joke he much regretted – that the rains would hold off until he had completed thatching his new house. Fear and accusation of neighbours and also of co-wives and others linked by marriage are quite common but in my own records close kin are those most often involved. Both men and women claim that the large majority of sorcerers are women but actual accusations seem to be much more evenly divided between the sexes. Fear of sorcery is a common motive for movement from one village or chiefdom to another, as I discuss in a later chapter.

The diviner and ritual expert (*mfumu*) is a key figure in Nyamwezi religious life for it is he, or occasionally she, who provides the all-important bridge between a cluster of beliefs and ritual action. The diviner interprets and harnesses 'the system' for an individual or group. He decides which forces are impinging on their lives in a particular situation and he then informs them whether, for example, a particular illness or other misfortune is the result of ancestral anger or sorcery or, again, perhaps of an attack by *swezi, migabo* or comparable spirits. Once he has identified the influence of such forces for those who have consulted him, he will proceed to tell them how the problem may be dealt with and he will give his clients detailed instructions about the form of ritual which is necessary. A second diviner commonly helps the person or persons so instructed in the actual performance of the ritual in question. In addition, diviners often provide medicines or their formulae for people who consult them. Two main sets of constituents are usually combined in such traditional medicines. The first consists of herbal and other ingredients which symbolically represent the client and the second, called *shingira*, contain ingredients which typically symbolise the character of the complaint. Although the logic of the local medicinal system is characteristically expressed in terms of symbolic association – e.g. baobab bark may be used in medicine to help a woman become pregnant because of the 'fatness' of the tree – some medicines do appear nonetheless to possess curative properties. Moreover, in keeping with the general openness of Nyamwezi culture, the use of hospitals and village dispensaries with their orientation towards 'western' medicine tends to complement rather than conflict with the recourse to traditional medicinal and ritual practitioners.

Divination itself takes many forms. The most common of these is chicken divination in which a young fowl is killed and readings taken from its wings and other features. The throwing of lots is also found and some diviners read from objects stirred around in water or interpret the form taken by a lazy-tongs device known as *kasanda*. Others claim to divine by smelling a small twig or other object on which the person for whom the consultation has been made has deposited saliva. A diviner is said not to be able to divine for himself or his own family, but he must consult a colleague. Diviners provide their services free to each other but ordinary people pay them for their consultations. In my experience, a diviner must first tell his clients why they have come to consult him before the consultation proper begins and a fee is charged. The fact that some of them gain considerable wealth from the profession testifies quite strongly to their skill.

Recruitment to divination is not in any strict sense hereditary and many diviners are not followed by their sons in the profession. Nonetheless it is quite common for individuals to take up the art if they

Diviners consulting over the death of a young woman in Busangi village. (They are examining a chicken they have killed for the purpose.)

suffer a misfortune which is diagnosed as having been inflicted on them by a diviner ancestor who wishes them to follow in his footsteps. Some such persons simply set about learning to divine through apprenticeship and never in fact practise. There are, however, usually a number of practitioners in any village, though only one or two of them are likely to be regularly consulted by a wide clientele. All of them engage in farming like their neighbours and they participate fully in the social and economic life of their village.

As is clear in the case of fears and accusations about sorcery, Nyam-wezi religion and ritual may divide people from each other in unhappy ways – though this, as we shall see, is not necessarily without any posi-tive value since it may encourage people to open up new areas for set-tlement. In many contexts, however, the religious 'system' serves as a unifying force which often manages to allow people to express their solidarity with each other without loss of individual identity. The most straightforwardly public rituals – sacrifices to royal ancestors or ceremonies to cleanse a local community of pollution following the death of one of its members – clearly affect considerable numbers of people *en masse*. Kin and neighbours, however, customarily also attend each other's personal ancestral sacrifices, life-cycle rituals and even ceremonies to exorcise unwelcome spirits, which also of course lead to the afflicted person's incorporation into an association of fellow sufferers as I have described, and this fits with a strong sense of the need in general to provide mutual support and encouragement at critical moments of joy, doubt, or misfortune in each other's lives. As my account implies, a great deal of religious activity is embarked upon in the face of specific tasks or problems and it would be quite wrong to underplay this tendency for ritual to be used to try 'to do' things in the Nyamwezi area as elsewhere.[7] At the same time one must recognise, however, that this 'doing' is not restricted to the purely practical, but also includes helping individuals to make significant sense of their lives and that Nyamwezi religion, like others, has an important moral and social component of which a theory of human powers for good and evil and a recognition of a mutual dependence upon others for support in crises are among the major, albeit partially implicit, features. Nyamwezi religion is concerned with human problems in the broadest sense of that term, and its ability to incorporate new elements which come within its compass – such as forms of divination or new cults, providing they themselves are tolerant – involves a refreshingly modest assumption that there is no monopoly of human wisdom in this sphere. Thus an important task of ritual is to render an often difficult life meaningful for people and to help them face it with the necessary confidence for coping with it, rather than to push them to believe in and assert a body of dogma in itself. I can well remember in this context a combination of pleasure and triumph on the face of Mayebele – an old friend and ritual expert who is now sadly dead – during the course of a ritual he conducted during my first period of fieldwork. A mother and daughter had had a serious quarrel and the daughter had sworn never to set foot in her parental home again. She returned once, however, and subsequently became ill, and the illness was diagnosed by a diviner as due to the oath which she had broken. The ritual I witnessed was held to try to remove the force of the oath (*kudahya mana*) and permit the resumption of fruitful relations between the daughter and her parents. The first part of the ceremony was conducted in the house itself – a second part involved 'casting away the oath' at a nearby forked path – and this was mainly concerned with the mother and daughter themselves. It took the form of a ritual, involving a combination of the use of medicines and symbolic gesture, aimed at bringing the oath under control and removing the hard feelings which had sullied the relationship between the pair. Towards the end of this first session, the girl broke down and mother and daughter clung to each other in a tearful and clearly heartfelt embrace of reconciliation. It was at this point that my friend turned round to me with the look of satisfaction I have mentioned and said, 'There. You see how effective are my powers.' Such ritual is partly 'practical' in its explicit aims – a person has been ill and the diagnosed cause of illness has to be dealt with as best it can – but it also clearly gives a moral meaning to the problem and pays close and valuable attention to the individual's ability to live at peace both with himself (or herself in this case) and with those who are dear to him. The value of attention to such problems is something which Nyamwezi religion and their society and culture generally tend to take for granted, and their attempts to combine the practical, the spiritual and the social in their dealings with illness, death and other afflictions is, as western society is beginning to appreciate, much less mistaken than a coldly analytic 'scientific' view might *prima facie* lead one to assume.

2 Political organisation: local government and justice in the national frame

Few anthropologists would try, today, to study local government and politics in isolation from their wider national or other political and economic environment. In the Nyamwezi case, indeed, it is quite probable that an exercise of this sort would have been of very doubtful value for much of the people's past history, and because of this I felt constrained to pay considerable attention to the influence of trade, colonial government and party politics in my earlier work on their political system (Abrahams, 1967a). Certainly, it seems clear that a closed and isolated study would be quite inviable in any rural region of contemporary Tanzania. In the period since Independence the many different parts of Tanzania have been consciously and carefully incorporated within a unified one-party national political framework centred mainly on the Party itself (TANU which in 1977 joined with Zanzibar's Afro-Shirazi party to form the CCM); and a central avowed aim has been to develop a strong system of participatory democracy in which government at all levels would truly represent and be responsible to the people. Looked at from this point of view, local politics in Tanzania are part of the national system and must be treated as such. On the other hand, it would also be mistaken to attempt to treat them simply as national-level politics writ small. For local areas, and in Tanzania this predominantly means local rural areas, have their own specific characteristics and interests and they also tend to lack the largely urban base and life-style and the well-developed bureaucratic structures which are typical of the main administrative centres of the nation, from Dar es Salaam and Dodoma down to most District headquarters.

In the account which follows I begin with a brief review of the former chiefdom system which I documented in the 1950s, and I go on to examine some of the new forms of political structure which have been erected in its place. The problems of nation-building which these new forms are aimed at solving are well known to be formidable ones;

26

and if my subsequent account appears to focus rather sharply upon them this is not because I wish to engage in unsympathetic criticism. Like many anthropologists I have come to care quite deeply for the many villagers and others who have generously received me into their lives. I realise, however, that I have no monopoly, legitimate or otherwise, of such concern and commitment, and I write simply in the hope that my discussion can contribute to an understanding of the issues in question which may be useful to both Government and people in their desire to develop and maintain the special combination of morality and political and economic viability which the nation's policies set out to achieve.

The demise of chiefship

At the time of my first visit to the Nyamwezi, chiefship was still their main political institution. Their country was divided into about thirty chiefdoms – their populations ranged from a few hundreds to a little over 70,000 – and each of these was under the authority of a chief and his subordinate headmen. The titles of these office-holders – *ntemi* (chief) and *mwanang'wa* (headman) – were traditional, and most of the chiefs and many of the headmen belonged to ruling dynasties and their constituent divisions which were well established in the area when Burton, Speke and other mid-nineteenth-century travellers first passed through their territories in search of the great lakes and the Nile's source.

But if chiefship was an old Nyamwezi institution, it had also for a long time been a changing one; and it seems clear that its transformations were in large measure engendered either directly by, or less directly in response to, the procession of external forces and contacts to which the area became exposed from at least the first decades of the nineteenth century. As I have mentioned, Nyamwezi trading visits to the coast around that time were followed by Swahili, Indian and Arab penetration of the Nyamwezi area, especially for the ivory and slave trade, and this in turn was followed by the arrival of Europeans in the form first of explorers, then missionaries, and ultimately colonising powers. German rule began in 1890, though not without resentment and resistance in some areas, and it lasted until 1916 when it was overtaken by the events of the First World War. It was succeeded by the period of British rule which ended in its turn with Independence in December 1961. In the course of contact with this long chain of external influences, Nyamwezi chiefship moved steadily away from the mainly ritual and somewhat insulated character which it seems originally to have had; and although it never wholly lost its religious and cosmological significance, in which the physical well-being of the chief was seen as connected with the well-being of his country, it became more and more vigorously involved in the temporal political and economic world. It was in the heyday of these developments, in the middle decades of the nineteenth century, that a number of extremely powerful chiefs emerged including Fundikira and, of course, Mirambo (cf. Bennett, 1971) whose extensive powers stretched well beyond the boundaries of his own chiefdom. By the beginning of the twentieth century, however, the process of secularisation had been accompanied under German rule by the casting of Nyamwezi chiefs, and their counterparts elsewhere, in the role of administrative subordinates and agents of the colonial power. The payment of tribute to the chiefs themselves was accompanied and ultimately replaced by the payment of tax collected by them for the wider Government they now had to serve, and more generally they became the mouthpieces and guardians of law and order in the rural areas for an alien regime. And as the Germans (and later the British) came to favour a rule of patrilineal succession to the chiefship – it had originally been matrilineal in much of the area though this had already changed indigenously in some parts – several men who were quite ineligible for the office by traditional criteria became chiefs under the new rules. It says much for the behaviour of the chiefs, and for the tolerance of their people, that chiefship retained as much dignity and legitimacy as it did during the colonial period, but it was partly consequent upon its colonial involvement, as I discuss below, that it was abolished as political office by the independent Government which took over from the British. There is some irony in the fact that this abolition was tempered by the announcement that chiefs could still perform, and be elected to perform, purely 'traditional' functions, by which was meant mainly the sorts of ritual duties with regard to crops and rainfall and the like which their predecessors had when they first envisaged the possibilities of a more secular political future for themselves a century or more before.

Two main factors seem to have contributed to the attack on chiefship after Independence. One was the simple but important fact that powerful hereditary offices were not easily reconcilable with the ideals of participatory socialist democracy to which TANU was committed. Indeed, it is clear that many chiefs anticipated that this problem would arise with Independence, and some of them tried, albeit unsuccessfully, to explore the possibility of a constitutional compromise which might combine democratic institutions with a safeguarding of their own status in the future nation. Thus much attention was paid at a special conference in 1959 to the question of whether the future constitution of the country could include provision for a second parliamentary 'house of chiefs' – more or less on the model of the English House of Lords – to complement a 'first house' of elected representatives; and one major Nyamwezi chief even became quite interested for a time in the idea of a federal constitution for the nation in which the local power base of chiefs might be more easily and legitimately protected and developed.

The second major factor was the force of the idea that the chiefs had been so intimately part of the colonial governmental system, since their participation in it had made them extremely vulnerable to accusations that they were a group of mere 'colonial lackeys', even though the real situation had been rather more complicated than such an accusation implied. As my own and other research on this issue showed, Nyamwezi chiefs and those in other areas were typically poised during colonial rule in a very delicate position between the European administration and their subject body, and it was apparent to most of them that their viability in office depended heavily upon their capacity to negotiate a path which did not give undue offence to either side. Some made serious mistakes in their attempts to do this and, as a consequence, alienated themselves from popular support. It is also true that a few took pleasure in exploiting the privileged position afforded by their access to the ear and backing of the District Commissioner and other central government officials, but it should be borne in mind here that these officials were themselves often anxious to protect the subject body from abuse of power by chiefs, and that many chiefs took their duties seriously and were equally anxious to provide good public service for their subjects. This included both the representation of their subjects' interests to the central government (for they were also a mouthpiece for the governed), and the provision of an efficient and relatively impartial system of law and order under the protection of which subjects could live and work and move in reasonable security and to which they could turn for the resolution of their disputes and the satisfaction of legitimate claims. The chiefdom courts in which most chiefs participated actively as judges were a

central and, in general, much appreciated and much used feature of
the system. Chiefs themselves rightly placed great weight upon the
value of the service which they rendered through the courts, and I have
heard them use this as an undeniable and convincing argument
against troublesome subjects, telling them that while they might be
willing to quarrel with their chief at the moment, they would come
running to his court for help if they had a dispute to be settled. More
generally it may be said that, despite individual frailty and the
complex pressures under which they worked, many chiefs took
seriously the admonitions which were customarily made to them at
their ceremonies of installation. There a new chief was told by the
main ritual elder of the chiefdom that he had no father and no mother;
all, even these, were now his 'children'. He should not hesitate to share
his food with any of his subjects and he should be just in court, neither
favouring the rich nor maltreating the poor. He should be ever
mindful and respectful of his subjects who were themselves admon-
ished to help and respect their chief.

As the movement towards political independence gathered
momentum in the late 1950s, the intermediary position of the chiefs
became particularly precarious. Central government had not yet
come to terms with TANU over the timing and organisation of British
withdrawal; and District administrators kept a sharp look-out for
any sign of disaffection among the chiefs who were at the same time
under growing pressure from below to declare support for TANU or
be branded as its enemies. Some chiefs resented the emergence of new
TANU leaders whom they saw as an unwarranted challenge to their
own hegemony, while others were more sympathetic but were often
afraid to show their hand. Many understandably tried to hedge. Thus
I heard one chief tell a meeting of his subjects that they should not ask
to see his party card. 'I am a man of in-between' he told them. 'Look at
my face. Its colour tells you that I am no kinsman of the Europeans.
My face is my membership card.' Another confided to me how he had
managed to entertain a party delegation so well that they could not
find an opportunity to present him with their potentially compromis-
ing demands without seeming impolite.

Meanwhile, as political uncertainty and tension mounted in the
country, legitimate government seemed for a brief period to be in
danger of collapse, and people began to resist, or reject outright, legis-
lation and procedures which might have been welcomed or at least
accepted in less difficult circumstances. Thus in the Nyamwezi area,

cattle-dipping schemes which were designed to control tick fever were opposed, and a few people even began to use *ad hoc* village courts instead of the official chiefdom courts to deal with offences like adultery, which were normally fully acknowledged to belong within the latter's jurisdiction. There were also tax-collecting problems in some areas, and in Ngaya chiefdom of Kahama District this erupted into violence and rioting which culminated in the chief's house being set on fire with the chief inside it. The chief was rescued by the District Commissioner and some police – the District Commissioner had himself been attacked earlier in the day – but his political career was at an end. This was, fortunately, an exceptional case and the general situation calmed down fairly quickly once rapid progress towards Independence was agreed between the central government and TANU's leaders. But the case for a fresh start in local administration was undoubtedly reinforced by conflicts between chiefs and subjects here and in such areas as Geita District, to the north, which were sparked off at this difficult time and were further fuelled and escalated in some cases by harsh words and errors of judgment on both sides.

My emphasis so far on the difficulties of chiefs should not of course obscure the fact that they enjoyed considerable power and privilege, and that the interstitial nature of their office also had its positive side. For although it was a source of trouble to them, it also helped ensure that chiefs were in important ways the best-connected persons in the network of relationships within a District. Admittedly there were social, cultural and ethnic boundaries between them and the 'District Team' consisting of the mainly European administrators and technical staff centred in the *Boma* (literally 'fortified enclosure') as the District headquarters were called. But there were few if any other Africans with equal or better access to this group. The District Commissioner's driver, Boma messengers and junior staff, and also some staff in the central offices of the Native Authority organisation which co-ordinated local government were comparably well placed in this regard; but they, like the District Team itself, were in the main less well connected than the chiefs in other ways.

For example, chiefs knew each other well, and there was considerable intermarriage between ruling families as well as links of shared dynastic descent between some of them. Many chiefs had gone to school together, for instance at Tabora School which had originally been founded as a training ground for future chiefs. Such school-tie connections helped to further chiefly solidarity, as did the more traditional inter-dynastic 'joking relationships' which many chiefs enjoyed acting out, with playful comments at each other's expense, when they met at official meetings or informal gatherings. There was also a great deal of intermarriage between chiefs and commoners, and the further fact that chiefs were in general by far the most active polygynists in the area – though this was not true of each and every one of them – helped to guarantee that their kinship and affinal links within their chiefdoms were much more numerous than those of ordinary subjects. This was typically further supported by the residence, despite migration, of considerable numbers of the members of a ruling family in its chiefdom, though it is true that such members were always a minority of a chiefdom's population and chiefs themselves were, at least at the height of their powers, often rather selective of the relationships which they were willing to acknowledge with distantly linked kin. As this latter point to some extent suggests, however, and in line with the admonitions in the installation ceremony that all his subjects were 'his children', a chief's connections in his chiefdom were not in any way restricted to those of more straightforward kinship and affinity, and many chiefs prided themselves on the wide range of their subjects whose characters, affairs and history were reasonably well known to them. Their long-term involvement in their chiefdoms and their administrative and other roles naturally facilitated the acquisition of such knowledge, but many chiefs consciously worked hard to get to know their subjects better, for example by extensive travel in both central and outlying areas of their chiefdoms.

In addition to its significance for the chiefs themselves, all this of course had quite important implications for the process of administration between villagers and central government, for it meant that relations between the two parties were mediated and cushioned by the chiefs who knew each side well and who, like Janus figures, truly 'looked both ways'. The chief's firm local base – the chiefdom was *his* territory in both a personal and an official sense – significantly complemented any more expedient awareness he might have of his dependence on the good-will and co-operation of his subjects, at the same time as he could never afford to forget the strength of the power exercised upon him from above and the advantages which he could derive from his connection to it. Most chiefs were in fact quite clearly more 'at home' in their chiefdoms than elsewhere, though one or two of the most widely experienced and formally best-educated among them seem, remarkably, to have been as comfortable among the silver and glass of a Governor's banquet as they were in sharing a common pot of beer or porridge with some of their poorer subjects.

Change, continuity and paradox

Chiefship was formally abolished as political office by the independent government in 1962–3, and new structures were created to replace it and the subordinate headmanships whose incumbents had served as the representatives of the chief's authority at the village-cluster and village level. The exact form of these new structures, and that of the District and Regional arrangements above them, is still to some extent in the experimental stage as changes have been introduced from time to time in such fields as village organisation (see below and Chapter 3), dispute settlement, and relations between local, regional and central government. Thus there was a process of 'decentralisation' of central government authority down to the Regional level in the early 1970s, and the definition of the key political and administrative units in the rural areas has been particularly subject to modification over the years. The basic elements in the structure, as opposed to their particular weighting *vis-à-vis* each other, have however remained relatively stable, and in this section I mainly describe, as an example of such forms and their implications, the situation which obtained in the Busangi area of Kahama District shortly after the first large-scale movements of the people into new villages in 1974–5.

Busangi was at this time the name of one of four Wards (*kata*) which combined to form the administrative Division (*tarafa*) of Msalala in Kahama District. The area covered by the Ward consisted of most of the fairly small chiefdom of Busangi which had existed prior to post-Independence re-organisation plus a few neighbouring parts of the former chiefdom of Ngaya. The other three Wards – Ngaya, Ngogwa and Lunguya – had themselves all been chiefdoms under the colonial system, though some boundary adjustments had been made since then; and they had traditionally been among the sections of an old larger chiefdom of Msalala which had been centred on Busangi and was broken up in German times when former headmen were made chiefs. The headquarters of the new Division, which had an area of about 2,500 square kilometres and an officially estimated population of 32,572 in 1973, were situated in Busangi together with the Ward's own offices, and the buildings used were, with a few additions, those which previously formed the administrative centre of Busangi chief-dom. Thus the old court house was still in use for dispute settlement and the former chief's house was now occupied by the Divisional Sec-retary (*Katibu Tarafa*) who was politically in charge of the Division.

The Divisional Secretary was appointed to the area by the Party from above, and he was clearly the most powerful official in the area. Despite the implications of his title, there were no formal Party or other committees operating at divisional level at this time, though these had existed earlier. Living next door to him was the Busangi Ward Secretary (*Katibu Kata*) who was similarly appointed by the Party from above and had a comparable role as chief political officer of the Ward. He was secretary of the Ward Development Committee (*Halmashauri ya Maendeleo*) and of the local Party Branch, for local Branches were now constituted at ward level. A second neighbour was the Magistrate who was in charge of the local Primary Court. Such courts constitute the lowest level of the nation's official court system – there are also other complementary forms of dispute settle-ment as we shall see – and this one served the Busangi area and had also served Ngaya for a time. In addition, there were a number of local administrative and technical staff who lived and worked nearby. The most high-ranking of these was the Divisional Co-ordinator (*Mratibu*), who was concerned with the implementation and dis-cussion of development and educational policy. A local veterinary assistant occupied a veterinary centre which had been built in a nearby village towards the end of the colonial period, and his wife also held office as the local Women's Development Officer in the area.

Below the level of the Ward were the villages (*vijiji*, sing. *kijiji*). Some people were still living in their old settlements – they were due to be moved later – but many had already been resettled into new large nucleated villages. These, like other settlements, were divided into Party cell units (*mashina*, sing. *shina*), each normally containing ten homesteads (*miji kumi*), and the elected leaders of these cells (*wajumbe*, sing. *mjumbe*) were to be combined into small-scale com-mittees who would send representatives to the Ward Committee. Such representatives would also act as local leaders of their village sec-tions. At that time, the arrangements for such representation were in a state of flux owing to the process of resettlement, but comparable forms had existed prior to village re-organisation and the office of *kinara*, as elected leaders of small areas of settlement were now known, had been created not long after Independence to replace the village headmanships which had formed the lowest level in the chiefdom hierarchy of offices.

Above the Division was the District (*Wilaya*) administration which was still mainly situated in the Boma formerly used by the British. Comparably, the houses which were formerly occupied by the colonial administrators in the area of Kahama town then (and still) known locally as *Uzunguni* (i.e. the 'European quarter') were now occupied by the representatives of the Independent Government who had succeeded them. The District structure, and indeed that of the Region (*Mkoa*) above it, was planned to be broadly similar to that on the Divisional and Ward levels. There was an Area Commissioner for the District who was a political appointee. He worked in co-ordination with a District Development Director, a Planning Officer and other technical and administrative staff to form a District Team and they existed side by side with the District Party organisation which had its own local elected Chairman (*Mwenye Kiti*) and its own offices in town. Similar arrangements were found at Regional level which roughly corresponded to the colonial Provincial level, though there are rather more Regions than the old Provinces and some Districts have been moved from one Region to another. Prior to Independence, for example, Kahama District was included in the Western Province centred on Tabora, but it was subsequently incorporated into a new Shinyanga Region centred on the town of Shinyanga to the east. Shinyanga District itself, which was also centred on the town, had for many years been part of the old and very large Lake Province, but the area had close cultural and historical connections with Kahama, which had in fact been administered for a time from Shinyanga in the very early days of British rule.

It will be apparent from my account so far that, notwithstanding the importance of the changes I have mentioned, these new arrangements manifest a substantial physical and spatial continuity with those they have replaced. This of course is natural and sensible enough. It would clearly be inordinately costly to scrap well-equipped existing buildings simply for the sake of having new ones; and the previous boundaries of territorial units, including chiefdoms and their subdivisions, were not simply traditional but also represented to some extent the demands of administrative convenience and efficiency, for instance in providing sufficient local courts and other services for people who still often have to walk or at best go by bicycle in order to make use of them. As such it would be wrong to attach a great deal of significance to such features in themselves, and it is necessary to pay further close attention to the much more complex patterns of change and continuity visible in the new formal structures of government and the personnel who man them.

An outline of the main structural changes has already been presented. It is clear that they constitute a radical attempt – though not a wholly successful one as we shall see – to provide through the one-party framework a unitary and truly unified replacement of the old colonial system with its rather sharp distinction between a central government (in that case controlled largely by expatriates) and the local rural population (mainly organised into 'Native Authorities' under chiefs). TANU was clearly pledged to this democratic aim and the Revolutionary Party (CCM) which grew out of its amalgamation with the Zanzibar Afro-Shirazi party is equally committed to the task, setting out among its objects the intention to ensure that 'by using the lawfully established forums, every citizen has the right to participate effectively in the national decision making process' and that 'all public affairs are conducted under the leadership and guidance of the Party'. The aim of incorporating the rural areas fully into the nation as a whole through the new structures is reflected in the choice of individuals who occupy the new positions of leadership within these areas. Thus the Divisional Secretary of Msalala in 1974–5 was a former school-teacher from a quite different part of Tanzania – the Shambala area in the north-east of the country – and his predecessor came from the Iringa Region in the south. The Ward Secretary was a young man and, like many others at this level of appointment, a Nyamwezi from a different part of the area who had been selected for the work by a District Selection Committee after showing himself to be a suitably devoted party worker. The Primary Court Magistrate was from the far south-east of Tanzania and he had previously been a Divisional Secretary, and still earlier a court clerk, before receiving special training in the administration of national and customary law for his present work. Neither he nor the Divisional Secretary could speak Nyamwezi and they conducted all their business through Swahili, the official national language, using interpreters if this was necessary. Other staff living in Busangi were mainly Nyamwezi from Tabora and elsewhere and none of them, with the exception of a Dispensary Assistant who was appointed when a new dispensary was started in 1975, had any particular connection with the former ruling family or with others, for that matter, in the place. The former chief had indeed left when his office was abolished and he was now living as a private citizen in Ngaya Ward, though it may be noted that this was not wholly typical since a number of chiefs had continued to reside in their old chiefdoms and some had even obtained posts at various times in the new system.

This last point deserves further comment since its significance can easily be oversimplified and misunderstood. In a paper based on data from the early 1960s, Norman Miller (1968) describes how certain Nyamwezi chiefs and headmen in Tabora District had continued to play a variety of political roles after the abolition of this side of their offices. Some had taken up official posts in the new structure while others had been able to retain a degree of unofficial and *sub rosa* influence. There was still some evidence of this phenomenon in Unyamwezi in the mid-seventies, though a number of those who were originally involved in the 1960s had by that time died or finally retired fully into private life. Thus one Kahama District chief was appointed as *kinara* in a new village in his former chiefdom after a period of retirement following a short period of service as a Divisional Secretary in another part of the District, and the son of a former chief I knew was a Ward Secretary. Moreover, as I shall describe in Chapter 5, some chiefs were involved in Government at Ministerial level in the early 1960s, and, although the amount of top-level participation has decreased since then, one chief and a chief's son are both Members of Parliament and have held a range of quite important offices over the years.

Two points should be made at once to begin to put such cases into perspective. The first is that such individuals are in a very small minority both at national and local level, since leaders are now regularly chosen from a much wider range of candidates than in the past. The second is that only some such people are involved today in public life and that, apart from any 'royal charisma' they may have, ex-chiefs and their sons constitute a reasonably well-educated and administratively experienced section of the population, so that it is not especially surprising if some of them should be chosen to put their talents to good use in public service in the new system. This said, however, it must also be admitted that chiefship has continued to be held in substantial respect by many though by no means necessarily by most Nyamwezi villagers. To some extent this seems to vary with the age of those concerned, since my impression was that older villagers were often more

Ancestral shrines (*makigabilo*). These belong to a former chief in the new village of Kisuke who still sacrifices for his former subjects.

conservative on this and other issues, despite the fact that many of them had keenly supported the move towards Independence. It may in part also relate to a succession of poor agricultural years which are said to have followed the political abolition of the office. Certainly, former chiefs are still quite often called upon to carry out rain rituals, and the fact that the Busangi chief had retired to Ngaya and had taken all his royal regalia with him was a source of some anxiety in this context to many Busangi villagers who would have liked to install someone who would come to live there in his place. In some areas, however, I was told that chiefs were also asked to settle disputes privately and were even consulted on a range of public issues by their former subjects; this indicates that secular as well as ritual considerations are to some extent involved in the situation.

Once again, neither too much nor too little should be read from this. Thus it is possible that at least some of the difficulties which the people have encountered are short-term ones of adjustment to rapid political and economic change, and certainly traditional chiefship seems to hold no longer-term solution to them. The relatively short period of time since Independence partly suggests this, especially when combined with the apparent influence of age which I have mentioned. Indeed it should be noted here that the Busangi area where I mainly worked seems to contain a somewhat higher proportion of older people than some other parts of the region – I discuss the reasons for this pattern in Chapter 3 – and this may well have coloured slightly the picture which I present in this section, as may the fact that I was visiting the area at an awkward time in 1974–5. On the other hand, it seems clear that there are still a number of more general and rather intransigent problems to be overcome if the full desired benefit is to be reaped from the replacement of expatriates and chiefs with leaders selected, as I have described, on national criteria of merit potentially from all sectors of society.

A main problem here has been that of achieving consensus and establishing effective communication between government officials and grass roots society at the village level. Admittedly, studies of local government elsewhere, such as Frankenberg's account of his Welsh *Village on the Border* (1957), to take a British example, help to make it clear that such difficulties are a very widespread if not an endemic feature of nation states everywhere. It is also true, however, that they are likely to be specially pressing in developing countries such as Tanzania, where most people live in rural areas which are as yet only imperfectly co-ordinated culturally, linguistically and economically into the nation as a whole. This is not to deny for one moment that the people of the country are intensely proud of being Tanzanians and entertain both deep respect and strong affection for their President, *Mwalimu* Nyerere. This said, however, it is also true that most of them are structurally bound to be preoccupied in much of their everyday life with relatively small-scale rural problems and affairs. One does find some exceptions of men who have moved out of rural life and, as it were, into the nation as a whole (see Chapter 5) and one must of course also take account of labour migration to coastal and other areas, and of the proximity of some villages to an urban centre like Tabora where many villagers have kin or friends. Such wider contacts are, as I have argued, an important feature of the 'openness' of Nyamwezi culture and society. It is true, nonetheless, that many of the longer-term hopes and ambitions of most Nyamwezi villagers still tend understandably enough to be contained within a relatively narrow rural framework, whereas this is, in the nature of things, much less true of those who lead and govern them; and this helps to create a situation in which despite Independence and their enthusiastic participation in the struggle for it, government still appears to many to be something which affects them from outside and from above.

It can be argued plausibly in this context that the very attempt at full political integration has paradoxically contributed to the problems it set out to solve. Partly this has happened in the course of implementing national policies within the rural areas, and partly it has hinged upon the patterns of recruitment to local and higher level administrative offices and their joint inclusion in a single national framework, as I have outlined. I should hasten to add here that some Government decisions such as the abolition of personal tax shortly after Independence have, not surprisingly, been very popular, and many people also appreciate the value of the introduction of free universal primary education for their children – though some baulk at its compulsory nature. Yet awareness of the benefits of a decision does not of itself create a feeling of active participation in the making of it, and less popular decisions tend of course to have the opposite effect. Two areas of governmental policy appeared to be particularly relevant in this regard in 1975. One was the re-organisation of local courts within a single national system which had followed the abolition of chiefship. The other was the enforced establishment of nucleated villages which took place in that and the previous year, and which naturally affected the political perceptions of the people very strongly at the time.

The re-organisation of the courts has, despite its laudable intentions, involved a regrettable double distancing between them and the people in the rural areas.[1] Firstly, the new magistrates are, like the Busangi one I met, typically strangers to the areas they serve and they do not seem to stay for more than a few years in a place. I shall discuss some further aspects of this more fully below, when I turn to more general matters of recruitment, but some important consequences should be noted at this stage. One is that a considerable amount of court business in the area is now conducted through a court interpreter translating back and forth between Nyamwezi and Swahili, though the need for this is decreasing. Another is that the magistrate, unlike many of his chiefly predecessors, tends to have relatively little knowledge of the people who appear before him, and although this fits more closely with bureaucratic ideals it can easily lead him to misjudge the guile or the experience of some litigants and witnesses which are quite well known to other participants and observers. Thus some individuals who are in fact quite fluent in Swahili can successfully pretend that they do not understand the language properly. I have also heard a magistrate somewhat patronisingly praise the high quality of the Swahili spoken by a witness who to him was just an aged villager but who, as I and many others knew, had in fact travelled to the coast several times and had a long experience of headmanship in the colonial period. It is easy to see how such misreadings can contribute to marking off a magistrate as an outsider, and one perhaps who is more likely to be manipulated and feared than respected.

The second problem with the local courts is that they no longer mainly administer genuinely local law and custom. The corpus of applicable national statute law has increased substantially in recent years and, in the case of marriage law for example, it is by no means always convergent with the premisses of local custom. Admittedly, the national law coexists with a variety of other rules at the Primary and District Court levels which concern most villagers. Thus there is a body of so-called 'customary law' which consists of norms endowed officially with regional and even wider standing, and there are also purely local rules which can be applied in an appropriate case. The broader 'customary law', however, is a somewhat artificial corpus which was put together in the course of a variety of governmental attempts to unify custom over as wide an area as possible, and the first steps in this difficult if not quixotic enterprise were, it may be noted, taken in the latter years of the colonial period.[2] Given its nature, a magistrate can be well versed in this form of 'custom', but he is much less likely to be aware of local customary details, and for information on these he typically has to depend on witnesses and assessors whose reliability he is not always in a good position to judge. There is some danger in this context, for example, that viewpoints of the older generation, from which assessors are most likely to be drawn, will be given undue weight in some types of case. I saw some evidence of this in a case where a young man who had run off with and impregnated a previously unmarried girl was ordered on the advice of 'knowledgeable' elders to pay to the girl's father an excessive combination of penalties, including a large sum for an allegedly customary named payment, *ngazigazi*, which had indeed previously existed but had fallen into disuse in that area. More generally, the very fact that there are different sets of rules, which are not all well known to litigants, and the further fact that they are chosen and applied in ways which can vary from one magistrate to the next, tend to make the Primary Courts appear increasingly to be something of a lottery to many local people, who still have to conduct their own cases – the use of advocates is forbidden at this level even if they are available – and who seem to have substantially less confidence than formerly that they can anticipate

41

what will be decided even when the facts have been established. This probably is even more the case with the town-based and more formally legalistic District Courts which now hear appeals from the Primary level. They have replaced the older appeal courts which were largely though not wholly manned by chiefs at the time of my first visit. It is of course in this general context of uncertainty that the occasional informal use of former chiefs for dispute settlement, which I referred to earlier, can most readily be understood.

It should be noted that the Government itself has been concernedly aware for many years of imperfections in the working of the courts, and it has paid a great deal of attention to them. One way in which it tried to alleviate some of the problems in this field was the establishment in 1972 of lower level and less formal 'reconciliation tribunals' (*mabaraza ya usuluhishi*) for handling civil disputes. These tribunals are potentially more satisfactory instruments of dispute settlement for many local people since the cases brought before them are heard by a panel of local 'judges', and their procedure and language – Nyamwezi is in common use at them – and the shared assumptions of those taking part in them combine to give them a much more home-grown air than the Primary Courts. The tribunals, however, are not courts – at least as far as Government is concerned – and as such they lack 'teeth' to enforce their recommendations. It is possible and fairly common for a disgruntled litigant to insist or, simply by inaction to ensure, that a case be reheard at the Primary Court. In such cases, moreover, the magistrate is likely, and indeed is technically bound, to refuse to pay attention to the proceedings and decision of the previous *usuluhishi* hearing, and in some cases this can be extremely frustrating to all concerned except of course the individual who has for better or worse reasons refused to accept the *baraza*'s recommended settlement. Thus in a case concerning compensation for adultery which I heard, the accused offender at first denied at the 'reconciliation' meeting that he had committed the offence, but he eventually agreed that he had done so after subtle and persistent questioning and being faced with a barrage of evidence, including a confession from the woman who became temporarily angry when he said something which seemed slightly disrespectful of her. The *baraza*'s recommendation was that he should pay 800 Tanzanian shillings (about £50 sterling at then current exchange rates) in compensation to the husband, and he appeared to agree reluctantly to this but in fact made not the slightest effort to pay. Eventually the husband decided he had waited long enough, and he took the matter to the Primary Court where the adulterer brazenly denied the offence once again and the magistrate refused to take account in the hearing of the fact that he had previously confessed to it. The adulterer eventually lost the case again, and the magistrate in fact handled it quite well, but all this had taken several months and with a less persistent and experienced opponent – the husband was a former chief – the culprit might have managed to escape unscathed from the affair.

These problems in the field of dispute settlement are interestingly compounded by some features of the situation with regard to the informal neighbourhood 'courts' which I found to be especially important in the villages of northen Unyamwezi during the colonial period. As I have described in detail elsewhere (1967a, Ch. 8), these courts which had traditionally complemented the more formal chiefdom courts became, along with neighbourhood co-operation in other activities such as millet-threshing, a focal point and indeed an instrument of conflict between villagers and their colonial masters as the struggle for Independence intensified. Some attempts were made to control them at the time, and one of these backfired awkwardly for the Government when some neighbours who had fined people for breaking a boycott on an Asian shop were charged with arrogating themselves the power of a legal court – they successfully appealed against conviction on the grounds that no official court actually had the powers which they had assumed! The fact that Government and TANU not long after came to terms about the independent future of the county helped draw attention away from such problems, and the exact status of the neighbourhood courts still remained unsettled after Independence. Certainly in 1974–5 people in Busangi were very unsure of the extent of their rights, if any, to hold hearings of this sort, and this emerged extremely clearly in the handling of a case of verbal abuse in the new village there. A local homestead head, who was well known over a wide area for his lack of self-control when drunk, insulted a local widow who then complained to their joint neighbours. A long discussion took place in which attention was drawn to a case a couple of years before. An offender had been told to pay a customary fine, *masumule*, and one of his kin – a politically ambitious man we can call 'M' – had complained to the then Divisional Secretary, the predecessor of the present one, who had informed the neighbours concerned, and it seems correctly, that they had no legally-recognised right to impose such a fine. When they argued that it was traditional to do so, the Divisional Secretary apparently made rather scathing comments about hearings of this sort more generally. Although the case did little to enhance the political reputation of the complainant – 'when that Divisional Secretary moved to another area, he "buried" M', one old man told me pithily – it did make people very careful for the future. In the present case the offender was eventually warned about his conduct but no fine was exacted. During the discussion leading up to this decision a number of speakers drew attention to the difference between central government, which they called *serikali*, and their own local customary concerns, which they referred to mainly in terms of 'elderhood', *bunamhala*, a term which is applied not simply to old age but also much more generally to the status of mature men who are established heads of their own households in a village. It was clear from these comments and from subsequent discussion of them that the long-standing contrast in this area between local community and state, which had earlier been a feature of the relations between neighbourhood on the one hand and chiefdom and wider organisation on the other, was still strong at this juncture. Moreover, it was highlighted in the present case by the accurate but also pointed shift from Nyamwezi to Swahili when the rough comments of the previous Divisional Secretary (from Iringa) were being recalled. I should add that provision does in fact exist within the Party structure for gatherings of Party 'elders' (*mabaraza ya wazee*) to take place at different levels and discuss matters of interest including disputes but they are not, I understand, entitled to fine wrongdoers. Not long after the above case of abuse arose the Divisional Secretary in Busangi in fact announced that he was going to try to set up such arrangements there, and it is possible that news of the case had in fact reached him at the time. How the system has worked out in practice since then is unclear, but it should be noted that the problems of divided 'jurisdiction' between such gatherings and the Primary Courts and of the contrast between small community and wider state, to which I have alluded, are deeply ingrained and not likely to be easily resolved. The fact that by no means all villagers are paid-up Party members is also a potential source of difficulty in this context in many areas (though exact figures are understandably not easy to obtain). I was told that this occasionally causes problems with the 'reconciliation' tribunals when some excessively zealous tribunal chairmen have been known to demand to see a membership card before agreeing to hear a case.

I will reserve my main discussion of the move into new nucleated villages until Chapter 3. Here it will suffice to note that these 'operations', as the Government called them, took place throughout the large part of Tanzania after a long period in which the majority of people had failed to respond effectively to official exhortations that they should set up comparable communities on a voluntary basis. A large proportion of the population were moved during 1974 and it was hoped that most of the rest would be moved in the course of the following year. Despite some cases of violence both from the governmental side and from the people in some other parts of the country, it appears that the 'operations' for the most part took place peacefully in the Nyamwezi area, though this does not mean that they were generally welcomed there. The moves created initial hardship for many and the Government's popularity was at a relatively low ebb immediately afterwards, so that I encountered a great deal of grumbling among villagers. The people had needed hastily to build new accommodation for themselves and their families in settlement patterns of which many of them did not approve. Their anxieties about living in close proximity with many others – fears of fire, epidemic and witchcraft loomed large here – were combined with a dislike of the inconvenience of living at some distance from their fields; there were also worries about whether the next step would be an enforced introduction of socialist collective (*ujamaa*) organisation for which there had so far been little enthusiasm in the area. It must be admitted that some people, and especially perhaps those who previously held relatively poor fields in some places, probably welcomed the re-organisation of the 'operations' as a possible opening to a better way of life. For most people whom I met at the time, however, their many anxieties seemed to be uppermost and to be only to a small extent allayed by the promises of better social services, for instance in the field of education, health and water supplies, which nucleated settlements were expected to make possible.

I have mentioned that the structure of administration and the patterns of recruitment to it have also been a source of problems. Taking the District level first, a characteristic feature of a number of the former European administrators is perhaps worth mention here since it was in part drawn to my attention by the comments of villagers who, I hasten to add, expressed no serious regret at their passing. For many of these expatriates, though admittedly much less so for their wives in many cases I have come across, the rural areas and 'open spaces' of

Africa had a strong romantic appeal, in at least short-term favourable contrast to the crowded, highly industrialised and urbanised society which they had left back home. Of course, they recognised that some Districts were more pleasant to work in than others, and some of the more remote and poorly supplied District Headquarters were sometimes spoken of as 'punishment stations'. It was clear, however, that these men often thoroughly enjoyed their 'foot safaris' into rural areas, the camping out, and the encounter with 'nature', as they liked to think of it, 'in the raw'. Such attitudes, and the extended visits to the rural areas which both fed and were supported by them, seem understandably enough to be much less common among modern administrators, who have in the majority of cases grown up in rural villages and have experienced for long periods the hardships and discomforts as well as the 'romance' of country life with an immediacy which their European predecessors might perhaps count themselves fortunate to have missed. Such men have left their villages for school or work in towns and most of them appear to value very highly the facilities available in even relatively small urban centres, such as hospitals, telephones, fairly well-stocked shops, garages, bars, and running water. These are things which they not surprisingly want to have more of rather than to get away from; and the fact that the prime focus of such men is likely to remain an urban one, until social services and other facilities in rural areas are substantially improved, adds to the danger of the development of communicative barriers between them and the rural population, who often remark that they are rarely seen for any length of time in any country area and that they rarely even pass a night outside a town.

Such attitudes to rural life, which cannot of course be weighed against the central importance of the fact that these men are Tanzanian nationals actively and committedly engaged in the development of their own country, are also to some extent apparent among leaders who are living in the rural areas themselves. The very nature of the old colonial idea of 'Native Authorities', and the distinction between their predominantly rural domain and the wider sphere of government controlled by European outsiders, meant with all its unacceptable faults that chiefs in that period were at the top of their own special ladder. This, coupled with their local aristocratic base and their complex integration into rural society, helped to generate a satisfaction on their own part with their role, and this significantly counterbalanced for them many of the difficulties they faced in their work.

Their modern administrative successors are, however, much less happily placed in this respect. Coming from outside, as many of them do, and holding relatively low positions in a national career scale, such men can all too easily come to conceive themselves imprisoned in a small administrative island of court house, offices, and official dwellings surrounded by a sea of local villages and their inhabitants with whom they tend to have, and are indeed legitimately entitled only to have, largely impersonal administrative relations. They typically lack local links of friendship, kinship and affinity which the chiefs enjoyed and, being subject fairly often to transfer from one area to another, they can do little to avoid this beyond participating awkwardly in public beer drinking or in sexual liaisons with one or more local women. The embarrassments which such activities may cause – a magistrate, to take a real example, having to deal with a case of two women who had drunkenly been fighting for his favours – are not hard to imagine. Nor is the situation of such men rendered any easier by the fact that many of them do not tend to see their marriages and homes as crucial sources of companionship and support in the face of the stresses and hardships of the outside world; and some of them may have their life made harder still by a wife's continued expression of her wishes to move into more congenial and if possible urban surroundings. For such men, then, promotion may be both a legitimate ambition for the recognition of their public service and a chance of escape from the role of perpetual stranger in a rural world; and it is scarcely surprising that many of them are keen to get it and unhappy at the thought that they might not.

These then are some of the factors in the modern situation, as I have encountered it, which have helped to lead many villagers to perceive government as something still external to themselves and rather outside their control. Admittedly, as I have noted, the time at which I found them was a particularly difficult one when the Government's popularity was running low owing to the move into new villages; and this was reflected, I was told, in the particularly poor turn-out at the combined *Uhuru* (Independence) Day and *Jamhuri* (Republic) celebrations which I attended in Busangi in December 1974. The main event was a procession in which schoolchildren, and the few adults including myself who cared to join them, marched carrying a framed portrait of the President to the Busangi Party headquarters singing a Party anthem '*TANU yajenga nchi*' (TANU builds the country), which incidentally uses the tune of an old Nyamwezi war song. This

Procession of schoolchildren at Busangi in December 1974 to mark *Uhuru* (Independence) Day.

was followed by a poorly attended meeting addressed by the Divisional Secretary. Some of the more general problems I have discussed were also visible at this meeting, however, when for instance the Divisional Secretary announced a little tactlessly that people should provide free labour to rebuild the latrine for a former TANU office building which was now going to be used as a Dispensary. No one informed him at the time, and labour was indeed drummed up next day, but some people felt he should have known that the building and latrine concerned had in fact already been built by public subscription some years before, and I heard some grumbles that the Party should not have allowed the latrine to get into the dilapidated state it had after it and the building had been provided in this way. Again, the election of ten-house cell leaders in Busangi in January 1975 was marked more by apathy than by enthusiasm on the part of both electors and elected in my own and several other cells. Although once again this may partly have reflected the immediate situation, I gathered that there was usually not much interest in elections of this sort, nor much temptation felt to try to participate actively in local politics more generally.

Before I go on to consider some more recent developments and some possibilities for the future, one particular structural recourse which is theoretically available to the people for the representation of their interests should perhaps be mentioned here. This is the representative role of Parliament (*Bunge*) and its members who are elected from the single-party framework from local constituencies. A number of factors make this a less practical recourse than might at first appear to be the case, even though it is clear that some MPs work very hard to try to help their constituents. Firstly, the population of a rural constituency is spread over a wide area, and this naturally militates against much direct contact between members and constituents. Secondly, even when allowance is made for variation in the zeal and personal effectiveness of individuals, the power of MPs has tended to be kept in fairly close bounds by the Party and it was in fact decided to curtail their number to one per District in 1974. This is in line with the formal Tanzanian constitution, which explicitly declares the predominance not of Parliament but of the Party itself and its tiers of committees as the main political institution of the nation. As such parliamentary representation seems unlikely to provide any major resolution of the issues in question and it appears that villagers will need to speak up for themselves more actively and more directly, as I discuss in the next section, if they wish to assert their interests more strongly.

It may be mentioned in this context that some features of voting behaviour in parliamentary elections since Independence suggest that at least some of the people themselves do not always place too great a weight upon its results. After an initial vetting by Party officials of a number of prospective candidates, two emerged to contest each constituency. One was allotted a picture symbol of a 'house' and the other a 'hoe'; the purpose of these symbols was simply to help non-literate voters to recognise the names of the candidates on the ballot sheets. Neither symbol in itself was expected to be more attractive than the other, and each was allotted in a complex system designed to randomise the allocation. At least in the 1965 and 1970 elections for which full data are available, 'hoe candidates' swept the board in Unyamwezi and in much of the immediately surrounding area. I leave a discussion of why the hoe was perhaps a more attractive symbol to the people until the next chapter. What may be noted here, however, is that many people seem to have cast their votes in favour of candidates whom they have apparently felt unable or unwilling to judge on the basis of their character or other personal qualifications for office, as opposed to which symbol they happened to have been allotted.[3]

Recent developments and the future

The picture which I have presented in the previous section relates mainly to the period in 1974–5 when I was again residing in the area. My information on developments in the period since then is not as full, but it is, I hope, nonetheless useful. It is based mainly on official documents, correspondence, and the material which I was able to gather on a further trip to Tanzania, including a brief stay in Unyamwezi itself, in December 1978.

One point which emerges about this most recent period is that morale appears generally to have been higher than I left it in the spring of 1975. People have begun to get more used to their new villages, though the system will need more than this to be successful (cf. Chapter 3); and although the war against Amin has been a cause of widespread hardship in the form of short supplies and rising prices, it does appear to have sharpened people's consciousness of themselves as proud citizens of a country engaged in an honourable struggle. Rainfall has also been quite good in some of the intervening years and this appears to have helped considerably to maintain a sense of fruitful purpose in the rural population.

Structurally, there appears to have been a potentially important shift of emphasis towards action at the village level. The 1975 Villages Registration Act provided for the official recognition of the country's newly established villages as multipurpose co-operatives, and efforts have been made to make the village a main political and economic decision-making unit. I will discuss some aspects of this in more detail in the following chapter, but it may be noted here in this context that the constitution of the new Revolutionary Party (CCM) stipulates that rural Branches shall be at the village rather than Ward level and makes no provision for other levels of Party organisation between the village and the District. Each Village Branch (*Tawi*) is expected to hold a Branch Conference (*Mkutano Mkuu wa Tawi*) at least once per year and to hold General Meetings of members (*Mkutano wa Wanachama Wote*) at least once per month. There is also a Branch Executive Committee (*Halmashauri ya Tawi*) which is expected to meet monthly. The Branch Conference is officially described as the supreme organ of the Party at village level and the list of its participants includes the following officers and categories of member:

Political organisation within the national frame

a The Branch Chairman ⎫   These are also Chairman and Secretary
b The Branch Secretary ⎭   of the village as a whole.
c The members of the Branch Executive Committee (see below)
d All members of the District-level Conference in the Branch
e All other members of the Branch

The Branch Chairman and six members of the Branch Executive
Committee are elected by the Conference at regular intervals. The
Branch Secretary is appointed by the Party from above. The Chairman and Secretary sit on the Executive Committee with the six elected
members, members of the District Conference group, and two
members of 'designated mass organisations' which may have sections
in the village. Examples of these last are the Youth Organisation and
the Union of Tanzanian Women. In addition to its electoral function,
the Branch Conference is in general charged with directing the implementation of Party policies within the village and it may form subcom-
mittees to facilitate this task. The Executive Committee has a number
of specified roles which include the explanation of Party policies to
members, monitoring membership applications and the behaviour of
existing members, offering guidance and supervision for all village development activities, and providing leadership in matters concerning
local defence and security. This emphasis upon the village level of
Party organisation was coupled with the abolition of the office of
Divisional Secretary, though this appears to have been only temporary, and the Ward level of administration has been maintained
throughout the period.

It is not easy to assess how well all this is functioning in practice. The
re-establishment of the Divisional Secretaries suggests that the new
arrangements have appeared to be unduly fragmentary to those co-
ordinating policy at higher levels; this is consistent with a further
recent development, the creation of a new category of externally
appointed officer, the Village Manager, who is supposed to help the
village in which he works to organise itself in useful and productive
ways. Not all villages have such Managers – Busangi, for example, did
not have one in December 1978 – and I was told that not all Managers
are properly effective. This may partly turn on the procedures of selection (I was told that Government departments and comparable bodies
were asked to release staff to fill many of these posts and they may not
always have chosen those they were most loath to lose), and the problems which I discussed earlier concerning the position of administra-

tive 'strangers' in the rural areas may also be relevant here, especially when such men have been transferred from urban postings. Whatever the cause, however, and although it is still rather early to attempt a firm assessment of the situation, it appears to be very likely that the 'managerial' system will be modified to take account of present difficulties.

Looking more generally to future possibilities, two developments would seem to be needed for the longer-term solution of the sorts of problems I have been concerned with in this chapter. The first is that the projected advance in the provision of social services and other facilities in the rural areas should in fact be realised so that the unwelcome gap in this respect between town and country can significantly be narrowed.

Secondly, it would be valuable if the people in the rural areas could genuinely exercise rather more control over their own lives; and it seems possible at least on paper that they might be able to do this through existing structural arrangements, especially in the light of the more recent emphasis on village-level activity. It would of course be naive to exaggerate the possibility of eradicating present problems in this way, since apart from any local difficulties there are almost certainly strict limits to the practicality of full popular participation in the government of any nation. It is however true that the Party system in Tanzania provides a framework, which is by no means present in all countries, for the people to try to play a more energetic role in decision-making than they did in my experience in rural Unyamwezi in 1974–5. At that time there were still, as I have noted, many people who were not paid-up Party members; and at least in Busangi most of those who were took little active interest in politics so that there was a tendency for many decisions to be made almost by default. Certainly it seemed possible in such an area for local Party committee members to be more active and more representative of local interest and opinion than they were. It could be argued from this that the typically heavy control which seems to have been exercised by appointed officials such as Divisional and Ward Secretaries at that time was, if only to a limited degree, of the people's own making; and, as I discuss in Chapter 3, it remains to be seen, to what extent the counter-argument that villagers' inactivity is actually an apt response to the realities of their apparent opportunities is tenable under the more recent conditions I have described.

Finally, a point I noted earlier may also perhaps be of relevance in this regard. I mentioned that it seemed that older villagers were often more conservative despite their previous participation in the Independence movement, and it must be remembered of course that some of them were already middle-aged when Independence was achieved. However this may be, the modern educational programme in which the young are all expected to receive at least primary education, which includes political education and the learning of Swahili, may help gradually to produce a rural population that is better equipped than its predecessors to take advantage of the democratic potentials of the new political system; the adult literacy campaigns which have been launched in many villages may perhaps help even to accelerate such a process. Without such a development, however, there appears to be a persistent and substantial danger that even official policies designed to make central government more accessible may misfire; and moves such as the greater decentralisation of administration down to the Regional level, which I mentioned earlier, and even the transfer of the capital from Dar es Salaam to the more centrally situated Dodoma, may have the unhappy and undesired opposite effect of appearing simply to bring the power of Government to bear yet more firmly on the people.

3 The village

Since Independence, village organisation in Tanzania has been an increasingly important focal point of the Party's and Central Government's attention, and Unyamwezi provides no exception to this general rule. The social and economic future of the nation has been seen, not implausibly, to depend on the proper development of rural society and its agricultural base; and some of the traditional patterns of village life, including those of mutual aid between neighbours which took place in Unyamwezi as elsewhere, were held by President Nyerere to constitute a firm indigenous foundation on which Tanzanian socialist development might be built. The attempts of the late 1960s to encourage the voluntary establishment of *ujamaa* socialist village communities partly reflected this view, at the same time as they marked a clear intent to move away from some existing forms of economic individualism in the country which were seen as an essentially colonial legacy. Thus, in his well-known essay *Socialism and Rural Development*, which followed shortly after his celebrated 1967 Arusha Declaration, the President wrote:

Our society, our economy, and the dominant ambitions of our own people are all very different now from what they were before the colonial era.... We have got rid of the foreign government but we have not yet rid ourselves of the individualistic social attitudes which they represented and taught. For it was from these overseas contacts that we developed the ideas that the way to comfort and prosperity which everyone wants is through selfishness and individual advancement. (1967a, p.4)

To counter this he went on to suggest that in a socialist Tanzania

... agricultural organisation would be predominantly that of co-operative living and working for the good of all. This means that most of our farming would be done by groups of people who live as a community and work as a community. They would live together in a village; they would farm together; market together; and undertake the provision of local services and small local requirements as a community. Their community would be the traditional family group, or any other group of people living according to *ujamaa* principles, large enough to take account of modern methods and the twentieth century needs of man. (1967a, p.16)

54

Such *ujamaa* communities were to be established through 'persuasion not force' and the first step would in many cases be to persuade people to move into compact settlements in which they could more easily perceive the advantages of collective economic activity and a socialist way of life more generally. In addition to re-asserting still desirable traditional values, the new communities would, it was hoped, also serve to overcome some less acceptable features of the past such as rural poverty and the inequality obtaining between men and women which were found in many traditional societies and which still persisted into modern times.

This influential essay was accepted as official TANU policy, and the *ujamaa* programme which followed in its wake was varyingly successful in different parts of Tanzania. In the President's report to the TANU Conference in September 1973, he announced that nearly 15 per cent of Tanzania's population were now living in some 5,556 *ujamaa* villages, but he pointed out that such villages varied considerably in the amount of communal activity within them, and their establishment was taking place at very different rates in different areas. In Dodoma and Mtwara Regions, for example, over half the people were said to be living in *ujamaa* communities, while in some other Regions, such as Shinyanga which includes Kahama District, less than 3 per cent of the people were involved in them.

The uneven pattern of *ujamaa* development seems to have contributed, along with possible external pressures, to a determination to speed up the movement of the population as a whole into new nucleated settlements, and this was expressed in the 1974–5 programme of compulsory 'villagisation' for the large part of the Tanzanian population. As I have already mentioned, large numbers of people were moved in both these years into new compact villages which, it was argued, would facilitate the desired processes of social and economic development through the provision of improved social services and the use of more efficient methods of agricultural production and co-operation. Since 1975 the new villages have been brought within the scope of a new Village and *Ujamaa* Village Registration Act. Through this they are first registered as 'multi-purposive co-operative villages' and the hope is expressed in an official 'guide' to the Act that they will in due course turn themselves into full socialist *ujamaa* communities. Basically, the President's original 1967 'first step' in the *ujamaa* process has now been compulsorily achieved over most of the country, though the move has been accompanied by explanatory policy statements, and the second step – to full *ujamaa* – has, in spite of some people's worries, remained to date in the voluntary sector.

The history of change in Nyamwezi village structure is not at all confined, however, to the post-Independence period, and it is perhaps of interest here that compact villages were also found in the mid-to-late nineteenth century when there was a considerable amount of local warfare in the area. Speke, Stanley and others have described the settlements of that period, and their descriptions tally well with those of old Nyamwezi I have talked to.[1] The main settlements, known as *limbuda*, were typically large and fortified, and they were often built in relatively inaccessible and rocky places. Commonly they were defended by strong wooden stockades, but occasionally stone ramparts were employed. They were usually inhabited by a chief or headman and some hundreds, and in some cases thousands, of his followers who cultivated fields in the surrounding countryside. Sometimes, smaller ancillary hamlets would be situated within easy reach of the main settlement whose protection would be sought in times of raiding.

Once peace was established in the area the need for such defensive units was no longer felt. People at first continued to live close together, but in rather smaller numbers, under the leadership of an *mzenga kaya* (literally 'the builder of the homestead') who was commonly the founder of the settlement. Such a settlement commonly contained as many as a dozen household heads and their dependants, and these household heads were in some cases, but by no means always, related to each other and the *mzenga kaya*. The settlement was usually surrounded by a fence or hedge beyond which lay the members' fields.

This pattern started to become less common after the First World War. Such settlements were usually built in the *mzenga kaya*'s fields and their site was usually changed after about ten to fifteen years. This was not unduly troublesome since huts did not last very long and had to be rebuilt in any case. There was, moreover, positive advantage to be gained from such a move since the plot of land on which a homestead has stood (*itongo*, plural *matongo*) tends, because of the household refuse which has been deposited on it, to be very fertile, but the advantage in this case was mainly for the *mzenga kaya* in whose fields the settlement lay. I was told that this was an important factor in the break up of such larger units, since individual men began to want to build for themselves and their dependants in their own fields and thus have the right to cultivate their own *matongo* when they moved their homestead site within those fields.

By the time of my first visit in the late 1950s the resultant form of relatively dispersed settlement had been prevalent for many years. Although occasional exceptions could be found, villagers typically built their homesteads in the area of land they cultivated, and this was bounded by the similar holdings of their neighbours within the same stretch of higher ground and under the authority of a local headman. The number of homesteads in such a dispersed village settlement varied greatly even within a single chiefdom, from as few as half a dozen to as many as a hundred in a large long-settled area, and in most parts of the country the homesteads of all but the smallest villages tended to form a number of loose clusters separated from each other by a hundred to four hundred yards of open fields. Most homesteads contained a man as head, his wife or wives, and their children (especially unmarried ones) plus an occasional and varied sprinkling of kin of the head such as a divorced or widowed mother or sister, a younger brother, and perhaps a sister's children.

This pattern continued into the post-Independence period with relatively little change until the so-called 'operations' of 1974–5, and it can be argued that it is in many ways the most 'natural' form among those to which I have referred. For although it certainly did not emerge and flourish in a political vacuum, as I shall try to make clear later, it was nonetheless rather more a result of the people's own expressions of their social and economic preferences than earlier and later forms of settlement over most of which they have had considerably less control. Because of this it will be useful to discuss some of the main features of these pre-1974 patterns in some detail before turning to discuss more recent developments.

Settlement patterns up to 1974: time and village structure

Before proceeding further, it is important to note at once that the 'natural' quality to which I have alluded is not necessarily something in the favour of these forms, since the local 'common sense' perceptions which provide their base may perhaps be relatively short-sighted ones which give excessive weight to individual as opposed to collective needs and to their short-term alleviation. This said, however, it appears that the patterns nonetheless reflect real difficulties, constraints and attractions which will not automatically disappear at the behest of governmental planning, and a careful study of them can be quite revealing of the complex nature of the problems of ecological adaptation in the area.

One important point emerging from the analysis of these patterns is that change in Nyamwezi villages has by no means been restricted either to the sort of large-scale structural transformations or to the micro-movements within fields so far discussed. For it can be shown that pre-1974 villages also had their own life-cycles of growth and decay which were closely associated with population movements of varying intensity from one village and one wider area to another. Such movement has, of course, been facilitated by the replicated distribution of law, order and public services which the chiefdoms and the units which replaced them have provided in the region; and it has also been encouraged by the rules of land tenure. In the chiefdom system the right to hold land was a basic part of chiefdom citizenship, but land was said to belong to the chief, and its allocation was administered for him by the village headmen. As I have mentioned, newcomers were typically welcome at both chiefdom and village level, providing land was available, as it often was, and they either received an allocation of existing fields in the light of their needs or they were given permission, in new settlements, to clear land. Land could not be sold, and fields left behind by people who moved reverted to the headman for redistribution. Claims to inherit fields were often treated sympathetically but it was stressed that there was no automatic right to inherit land, and the chiefs and headmen reserved the right to lay down all sorts of conditions about the way in which a particular holding might be inherited. In short, the chiefdom system of land tenure provided considerable security of individual land use to the commoners who formed a substantial majority of any chiefdom's population, but it denied them any clearcut rights to pass on holdings to their heirs. This discouragement of the establishment by commoners of corporate land-holding kinship groups was, moreover, substantially maintained in the administrative structures which replaced the chiefdoms, since the new territorial authorities more or less took over the legal, though not the ritual, powers and functions of the chief and his subordinates in this regard. Some selling of fields began to take place in the period after the demise of chiefship, but it was a relatively transitory phenomenon, in part reflecting the uncertainties of change, and it appears to have been technically as illegal then as it was under the chiefs and, indeed, as it is today.

An important general feature of the population movement of this period was the tendency for individual men and their households to migrate to new places of their choice. Admittedly, some areas of western Unyamwezi were closed to settlement by the colonial government, who moved the population from them into closely bounded zones as part of the attempts to control sleeping sickness in man and animals. More usually, however, even when large numbers of people were migrating, as in the heavy inflow of Sukuma into Kahama and Nzega Districts since the early 1950s, they did so on the basis of their individual decisions. This in turn contributed significantly to the mixed nature of most village populations, which still often include people from many different places and from different Tanzanian groups. With the main exception of relations between members of the local ruling family, who were usually in any case in a minority, the network of kin ties in pre-1974 villages was typically rather loosely meshed and most homestead heads had few if any kinship ties to each other; and the further fact that intermarriage between fellow villagers was not especially common – though it was not directly prohibited – helped to perpetuate this situation. Consonant with all this, most Nyamwezi villages of the time could usefully be thought of as aggregates of individual homesteads between which there was considerable collaboration but whose members, singly or as household groups, felt free to move elsewhere should they so wish.

The village of Butumwa where I lived for part of my first fieldwork illustrates some of these features. The village had been started in the 1920s and in 1959 it contained thirty-nine homesteads, of which two belonged to a polygynist who kept his wives apart. The siting of homesteads *vis-à-vis* each other in the village can be seen in Figure 1. The ethnic affiliation of the homestead heads was Nyamwezi 26, Sumbwa 6, Sukuma 4 and Tusi 2. Six of the Nyamwezi, who represented the local ruling family, had been born in the vicinity. The rest (both Nyamwezi and non-Nyamwezi) had come at different times from a variety of places. Thirteen had no kin or marriage ties with any other homestead head, and few others with the main exception of the ruling group had more than one such tie.

When I returned to the area in October 1974, I found that many of these homestead heads were still alive, though some had moved to other parts of Kahama District and beyond. Those who had remained, along with others from surrounding villages, had been moved a few months earlier into the new large nucleated village of Busangi. It was, however, possible to reconstruct the situation just

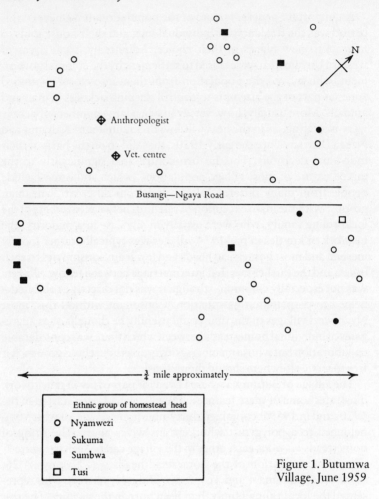

Figure 1. Butumwa
Village, June 1959

before resettlement and to obtain a picture of Butumwa's development up to that time.

Tables 3.1 and 3.2 provide data on the age and whereabouts of 35 of the 38 homestead heads of 1959. All 35 were married men and the other missing three consisted of (1) an old woman who was temporarily in charge of a homestead and is now dead, (2) a middle-aged Tusi who was in many ways marginal to the community and is now dead, though his son is still about in the area, and (3) a middle-aged Sukuma

Table 3.1: Butumwa homestead heads, 1959

Age in 1959	Under 30	30–39	40 plus
Number in 1959	6	2	27
Alive in 1974	6	2	17
Still in Butumwa in 1974	1*	1	13
Died in Butumwa by 1974	–	–	7
Alive elsewhere in 1974	5	1	4
Died elsewhere	–	–	3

*This man was a Roman Catholic catechist who worked for the nearby mission at Ngaya.

who came in the late 1950s but left without trace shortly afterwards.

Table 3.1 roughly divides the thirty-five according to their age in 1959 and tells us something of their subsequent history. Table 3.2 provides more data on the 40 plus age-group. I have divided their ages into three categories (a) 40–49, (b) 50–59, (c) 60 plus, and I have assigned slightly uncertain marginal cases to mixed categories. One point which begins to emerge from these tables is that, even allowing for some growth in population (see below for data on the effects of internal growth and immigration on the number of households), there was a substantially larger number of Butumwa homestead heads who

Table 3.2: Butumwa homestead heads aged 40 and over, 1959

Age in 1959	(a) 40–49	(a/b)	(b) 50–59	(b/c)	(c) 60 plus
Number in 1959	5	8	9	3	2
Still in Butumwa in 1974*	4	5	3	1	–
Died in Butumwa by 1974	–	1	3	2	1
Alive elsewhere in 1974	1	–	2	–	1
Died elsewhere by 1974	–	2	1	–	–

*The age groups of these men in 1974 were (a) –, (b) 2, (c) 11.

were clearly over 60 years of age in 1974 than there had been in 1959. Another point is that although there seems to be no clear trend for members of particular age-divisions over 40 in 1959 to have stayed or moved, the fact that five men moved who were in their fifties or just under at that time may be significant, as I will explain below.

Many of the 1959 homestead heads had sons or other male dependants, such as younger brothers, who either had their own households then, within the same homestead, or acquired them as they grew up and married between 1959 and 1974 (cf. Chapter 4, pp. 176–8). My information on such people is not as full as I would wish but the situation with regard to them appears to be as follows. Firstly, some such people, though I believe not very many, had already left the village before 1959. Secondly, of those there in 1959, twenty seem to have stayed on in the village and nineteen left. Nine of those who stayed already had their own households in 1959 as had five of those who subsequently left. In at least four cases, those who left took the homestead head *with them*, rather than vice-versa. It is in this context that the migration of four of the five (a/b) and (b) cases in Table 3.2 which I noted above may be significant, since these were in fact the four cases in question and their moving reflects the needs and interests of their junior dependants at least as clearly as their own.

In addition to the homestead heads of 1959 and their dependants, there had also been eight newcomers to Butumwa between then and 1974. One of these was over 60 when he came to marry an old woman who was living in the village, and another lived there only temporarily while he held a job at the administrative headquarters a couple of miles away. Of the remaining six, four came with adult sons, though it is not fully clear who brought whom in these cases. One of them left fairly shortly afterwards with his sons, two others were eventually left behind by their sons who went on elsewhere, and the fourth, who came from a neighbouring village to take over the usufruct of his dead mother's brother's fields, was still there in 1974 with his son. The remaining two newcomers were still there in 1974. One was a younger man who came simply to a vacated plot, and the second, who was also relatively young, came to join his brother-in-law after his own father's death.

Although the above material is not conclusive in itself, it does suggest that between 1959 and 1974 the village had begun to reach a crucial stage in its development, and this view is supported by informants' statements and by case material. The village appears to have become what one might call a 'saturated' settlement which was begining to experience significant out-migration. The number of households within it was, admittedly, fairly close to that of 1959, but it had been losing many of its younger members and there was now a substantially larger contingent of old men than there used to be. What would have happened to the village had it not been overtaken by the special events of 1974 is not absolutely certain, but some clues are, I believe, provided by the decline of the neighbouring village of Kibama which was more or less empty by 1974. Kibama had been started earlier than Butumwa, and in 1959 it had a rather larger proportion than its neighbour of elderly homestead heads. Most of these had died by 1974. Few of them in fact had children, but in any case scarcely any of the younger members of the settlement in 1959 had stayed there and those who did seem to have had special reasons. Thus three of them had shops in the nearby shopping centre which served the local administrative headquarters and enjoyed a sizeable passing trade.

Returning to Butumwa, the main reasons which people advanced to explain movement away from the village are similar to those reported for the neighbouring and of course related area of Sukumaland.[2] Witchcraft fears, relative land shortage – exacerbated now by the development of cash crops – and a partly consequent perceived decline in soil fertility were among the central factors pushing people out, while knowledge and rumour about other, often less developed places in which land was both more plentiful and fertile served at the same time to attract people away. The following three cases which I have chosen from a number of possible examples furnish fairly typical illustrations of the sorts of processes involved. At the same time they provide some interesting and useful hints about the ways in which ecological adaptation and the exploitation of resources in the area appear to have been tied in with social structural factors such as the developmental cycle of domestic groups.

Case 1

The first case concerns a man whom I call Kulwa, his wife, and some of his children.[3] Kulwa was about 50 years old in 1959 and was married then to his present wife whom he married in the early 1940s. This wife was his sixth, and he has had ten wives altogether. He has tried to establish polygynous households at various times by marrying this and later wives, but the others have simply fallen by the wayside since his present wife can be a rather difficult person. In 1959 Kulwa's

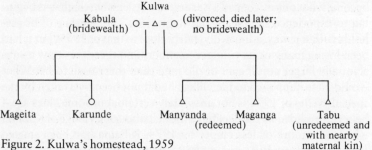

Figure 2. Kulwa's homestead, 1959

homestead was as in Figure 2. It should be noted that children of non-bridewealth marriages (see Chapter 4) customarily belong to their mother's kin unless redemption payments have been made for them.

None of the children was married although Manyanda, the oldest, was in his late teens and was hoping to marry soon. By the time I returned in 1974, Kulwa had redeemed Tabu, who had been living with a matrilateral kinsman nearby, but both he (Tabu) and Manyanda had gone to live in another, more fertile part of Kahama District. Maganga had established his own separate homestead not far from Kulwa, and Mageita had married and had a household within Kulwa's homestead. Karunde had also been married by that time.

Mageita's and Karunde's mother, Kabula, is seen by local people as a key figure for the understanding of many of these events. Manyanda, who had married in 1962 and has had several children, left in 1971 because his crops were not doing sufficiently well for his needs, but there was it seems also a feeling that Kabula was in some way personally to blame for this. Shortly afterwards, Tabu also left and went to join Manyanda. Tabu had, it seems, been redeemed with part of the bridewealth which Kulwa had received for Karunde when she married, and this appears to have caused ill-feeling since the separate identity of different 'houses' in such multiple domestic structures tends to be jealously guarded not least by the wives and mothers concerned. Eventually Mageita became ill and Kabula is said to have accused Tabu of causing this, telling him apparently that if her son Mageita died, he, Tabu, had better eat the corpse. Shortly after this remark, which was tantamount to an accusation of witchcraft, Tabu's house caught fire, and he then left to join Manyanda.

Case 2

A second case concerns a former neighbour of Kulwa – a man I call

Mabula who was also about 50 years of age in 1959. At that time his homestead had contained himself, his wife, and two of their three children. The third and eldest child was a girl who had already married and was living elsewhere with her husband. The two children at home were a second daughter, temporarily estranged from her husband, and a son, Mihayo, who was just about to marry. Also in the homestead was the young Tabu – mentioned above in Kulwa's case – since Mabula was a maternal relative of his and had been chosen as a suitable guardian for him until he might be redeemed. Some time after I left, Mabula's wife died and then in 1971 two of Mihayo's young children died within a single week. These last two deaths were, I was told, ascribed to witchcraft arising from a quarrel which Mihayo had had with a neighbour, and this finally pushed the group to move. Mabula, whose eyesight had deteriorated seriously in the last few years to add to his troubles, followed his son Mihayo rather than vice-versa. They moved to a place about 30 kilometres away called Masabi. In 1959 this had been a thinly populated though potentially fertile area. By 1974 it had become quite densely settled by Sukuma immigrants and others like Mabula.

Case 3

The third case concerns yet another neighbour of these men, a man I call Bundala, who had originally settled in Butumwa in the late 1950s conveniently near to Kulwa and his wife, Kabula, who was in fact Bundala's sister. Bundala was away for much of the next few years as a migrant labourer, and returned to settle down in 1965. After two years, however, he left Butumwa and moved to a more fertile and less crowded area in the south of the District. Bundala's homestead in 1959 contained himself, a divorced sister, his mother, his wife, a teenage daughter and three young sons. He also had a second wife whom he was just about to bring to Butumwa from the area in which he previously had settled. Between 1959 and 1967 when he moved, Bundala seems to have experienced a deterioration of his economic situation in Butumwa. One reason for this was that the ratio of working hands to mouths in his homestead became worse as his mother died, his sister remarried and moved, and his daughter had a series of babies by men who did not marry her. These problems of domestic development were further aggravated, it seems, by the decreasing fertility of local soil and by some partially related changes in agriculture in the area. These consisted of the development of cotton cash-cropping and the related change-over from the production of bulrush millet to that of maize (see Chapter 1) and it appears that Bundala's fields were rather less well suited for maize, a greedier crop than millet. It also seems clear, however, from other evidence, including that of Malcolm (1953) on Sukumaland and some of my own earlier collected data, that, important as they have without doubt been, these agricultural changes have nonetheless simply tended to accelerate rather than actually to generate the processes of village development and decline which appear to have been long intrinsic to the settlement patterns in the area.

These cases, then, provide an illustration of the sorts of processes which have been at work in people's movements from one locality to another. Before presenting a more general picture of them, however, I would like to give some further information on the age structure of a somewhat wider area of which Butumwa was a part, and to compare this with the population of a much more recently settled locality in the south of the District, together with a corrected version of the official 1967 Census of the District. My first set of figures were collected in a sample of 123 male plot-holders in the new village of Busangi which contained the populations of Butumwa and several other nearby villages. Every married man was entitled to a plot, and my figures show that thirty-one or 25.5 per cent of my sample were 60 years of age or more.

Turning from these figures to those for Kahama District as a whole, one finds that according to the 1967 Tanzanian Census, 21.6 per cent of the male population over 20 were counted as being over 60 years of age. Taking these figures at face value, the Busangi figures cannot be claimed to be very significantly different, but there seems in fact good reason not to do this. The official report on the 1967 Census (Volume V, p. 87) acknowledges the difficulties of assessing age accurately in national census-taking conditions, and it goes on to note that this census appears to have suffered from distortion as a result of these difficulties. The Census Report adds that the distortion in question is likely to be similar to that described in a 1968 Unesco document on the problem, according to which there is a strong tendency in such censuses to exaggerate the age of male respondents, so that probably 75 per cent of men in any five year age-group over 60 should be placed in the next lower five year group. If this correction is made for the Kahama figures, the relevant proportion would be 17.9 per cent, and the Busangi figures appear fairly significantly different, with a comparison of the numbers involved yielding a chi-square figure of 4.48 (significant at the 95 per cent level) with one degree of freedom. It should perhaps be added that my own data from Busangi seem much less likely to need such correction since they were collected jointly and rather carefully by myself and my field assistant, who was well acquainted with a considerable number of those interviewed and had a detailed knowledge of much local micro-history.

However this may be, the figures are by any account in violent contrast with those which I collected in the village of Kisuke in a fertile and relatively recently settled area in the south of the District. There, in a sample of fifty-four household heads, I found only one man over 60 years of age, despite the fact that there might well be more tendency for me to over-age respondents in a settlement where the inhabitants were not well known to me or my assistant. My figures for this settlement differ sharply from the District Census data and, of course, in the opposite direction from that of the Busangi figures. Even if one includes two senile men living as dependants, one obtains a minimum chi-square of 6 (significant at the 97.5 per cent level), with one degree of freedom, against the corrected Kahama figures, and this becomes a maximum of 12.4 (significant at the 99.9 per cent level) if one does not count these two men and makes the contrast with the uncorrected Census data. In either case, the discrepancy between the Busangi and Kisuke figures is a clear one.

Such variation between the age structures of different local communities is of some interest. Despite a scarcity of information on the topic (see however Swantz, 1970), it seems very probable that such differences form a regular feature of the population distribution of this and comparable parts of Tanzania – I obtained some confirmatory data on this for Nzega District in December 1978 – and they strongly suggest that large areas of Unyamwezi and beyond, which can all too easily be seen as aggregates of many individual and similar self-perpetuating villages, need in fact to be conceived as single and 'organically structured' ecological and sociological zones whose parts are interlinked by a complex pattern of migratory movement.

Having presented and commented upon a variety of numerical and case material, I want now to construct a more coherent picture of the form and implications of the processes of village and domestic group development which appear to have been intrinsic to settlements before 1974. Up to that time, Nyamwezi villages were, I suggest, processual phenomena in a number of important ways. Firstly, they tended to pass through a process in which their size and structure, and especially in this context their age structure, were changing over a number of decades. This process may be characterised as one of growth, saturation and decline and it seems likely, *ceteris paribus*, to culminate in an old village with a relatively old population, though the process does not simply correspond with the life-cycle of the oldest members of the village. This last point is related to a second way in which such villages were typically changing over time, that is through change in their actual personnel as a result of births and deaths and of the cumulative in- and out-migration of individuals and domestic groups.

These tendencies to change of size and structure and of personnel in villages appear to have been intimately related to a further range of factors and processes which are themselves interestingly consistent with each other. One such factor is that of environment and ecological adjustment to it, and one of its main features is the fact that, at least under customary techniques and patterns of land usage, Nyamwezi soils gradually become worn out. My understanding is that the deterioration of such soils is likely to take place simply through regular use with these techniques, but it seems clear that the process has, as I have mentioned, been somewhat exacerbated in recent years by an increase in cash-cropping and an accompanying decrease in labour migration. In addition, and more generally, it may be noted that the process seems likely to have involved its own intrinsic phases of acceleration inasmuch as demands on a village's cultivable land are in any case likely to increase in intensity, at a rate varying with that of population growth, during a considerable period of its history as the number and the size of its constituent households expand.

This last point draws attention to a further major factor in the situation, namely the developmental cycle of family and domestic groups. The legal and social status of these groups as component elements in the village communities under consideration is itself of some significance, as I will try to show in a later stage of my discussion, but there are some features of their internal structure and development which I wish to bring out at this juncture. Firstly, we may note that the period or phase which Fortes (1958) has characterised as that of the 'expansion' of domestic groups seems to be doubly geared in this area to the encouragement of population movement. On the one hand, if the processs of expansion is successful, the increase in the number of young mouths to be fed will tend to place an extra strain both upon land held by the group, as I have mentioned, and also of course upon labour; and such strain is likely to push people to seek more productive land elsewhere, particularly in the later history of a village. On the other hand, any failure in the expansion process through infant mortality is liable to generate fears and conflicts about witchcraft which also tend to push people away to new settlements. This fits well with the more general point, whose local-level political relevance has been stressed more often perhaps than its economic significance, that not only is the incidence of witchcraft accusations to some extent structured by the relationships between accuser, victim and accused, but also that the points at which such accusations occur in an individual's life-cycle and in the development of his or her domestic and other groups are themselves by no means randomly distributed.

A second relevant feature of the development of domestic groups is the high divorce rate in the area (see Chapter 4). This not only affects the residence of spouses inasmuch as a divorced wife commonly goes to live with kinsfolk in another village – and indeed a large proportion of marriages take place between members of different though not always very distant villages – but it also seems to have less obvious though no less serious repercussions on relations between fathers and their sons. As my field assistant shrewdly observed to me, it is unusual to find an adult son still living with his father in one homestead if his mother has been divorced. It would probably go beyond the limits of my fieldwork data to demonstrate this point statistically, but my material does bear out just some of the many factors which may conspire to make such co-residence difficult and to push sons to move away. In addition, it may be noted that it is not at all uncommon for a man to look after his divorced or widowed mother if she has not remarried, for example in old age, although this in turn may lead to difficulties, including the possibility of his divorce if his mother and his wife fail to get on well together.

The various ecological and developmental factors which I have outlined above have, I suggest, regularly combined to drive or at least tempt young and middle-aged men to move away with their wives and children from the villages in which they have been living, and the attraction of other and if possible more fertile parts of the country seems to have been at its strongest for them at the sorts of junctures I have described. I want now to complement this discussion of such 'statistical' processes with an examination of some more qualitative and more positively normative features of village organisation which have been interestingly consistent with and to a varying extent reinforcing of the processes in question. I have already discussed the role in this context of the wider political system in which villages were embedded. It remains, however, to examine also certain features of the customary forms of neighbourhood co-operation and mutual responsibility obtaining between fellow villagers in the area. My discussion of these will serve both to complete my account of 'traditional' settlement patterns up to 1974 and to provide a bridge to subsequent discussion of more modern village-level developments.

Customary patterns of neighbourhood co-operation

Even at the time when chiefship flourished as the dominant political institution in the Nyamwezi area, neighbourhood relationships and obligations existed as a relatively egalitarian field of social structure which was distinct from and mainly complementary to the more hierarchical set of ties between chiefs, headmen and subjects. The importance and scope of these neighbourhood relationships has varied from time to time and place to place, and during my first fieldwork they appeared to be most strongly developed in Kahama District. There, as I have described in greater detail (Abrahams, 1965 and 1967a), neighbours customarily co-operated in a large number of practical and ceremonial activities ranging from cultivation, threshing and housebuilding, on the one hand, to weddings, funerals, sacrifices and divinatory inquests on the other. They also recognised the shared obligation to respond to cries for help in an emergency. In addition, as I noted in the previous chapter, they participated in a well-developed system of informal local courts or moots which came into some conflict with the official Chiefdom Courts towards the time of Independence, when neighbourhood ties began to serve as a grass-roots base for TANU's opposition to colonial rule. The decisions of these 'elders' courts', as they were called, often involved fines of food or drink for communal consumption and they were backed by threats of ostracism (*bubiti;* literally 'hyenahood') against recalcitrant offenders. The offences they normally dealt with included minor cases of abuse and assault, the commission of mistakes at communal rituals, and failures to fulfil one's obligations to co-operate in neighbourhood activities. This last was customarily extended to include the failure to join at least briefly in the communal activities of other villages one was visiting or passing by.

Such then, briefly, was the situation in Kahama in the 1950s. In the other area of Unyamwezi I knew well, i.e. in villages around Tabora, co-operation took a more diluted form at that time. Labour was quite often hired to do work done by neighbours further north, and neighbourhood court hearings were less common. People were expected to join in each other's funerals and weddings but the failure to do so, I was told, would simply evoke a refusal to help in the offender's own ceremonial activities rather than an attempt to fine him and to ostracise him if he would not pay. Even in this area, however, the very word for 'neighbours' was evocative of a tradition of more intensive collaboration between villagers. For here, as in the north, they were called *bazenganwa*, a term which embraces both the active and passive notion of people 'who are built for, by and in the company of each other'.

Since the late 1950s the intensity of customary co-operation between neighbours in the Kahama area has tended to move more closely to the pattern that I witnessed in Tabora, and I shall discuss such modern developments later in this chapter. The main point that I wish to make about such co-operation at this juncture, however, is that it was and, as far as I can tell, still is conceived by the people themselves as based on the type of mutual obligation which has sometimes been termed 'balanced reciprocity' (Sahlins, 1965). Thus, as I myself described in 1965, people characterise ties of neighbourhood by reference to a notion of 'debt' which they see as seriously different from the obligations between kinsfolk. Kin should help each other when and how they can. Neighbours in contrast have an obligation in customarily defined contexts to try to give a more or less exact return for what they have received, and – as with Sahlins's concept – there is also a temporal aspect to this. This last point is well brought out by H. Mapolu, a Tanzanian and, indeed, a Nyamwezi sociologist (Mapolu, 1973). Examining the various local cultivation groups which have been customary among the neighbouring Sukuma, as in several parts of Unyamwezi, Mapolu emphasises how the various neighbours and friends who typically constitute such a group always co-operate on a strictly season-by-season basis. The groups commonly cultivate the fields of individual members in rotation for a small fee or subscription and they cultivate for non-group members for a larger fee. At the year's end, he describes, takings are pooled and used to buy meat and drink for a feast. Normally no balance is carried forward to the next year when a similar group, not necessarily with exactly the same membership, has to be reconstituted from scratch. Mapolu's interests in and conclusions from this data are only partially coincident with my own here – he is keen to show that such indigenous patterns are a poor base for socialist development and therefore have to be replaced by radically different longer-term forms of co-operation, as indeed seems to be happening in some areas. It is clear, however, that his point about the temporary nature of the collaboration in question fits well with my general picture. For although it is true that neighbours play a major role in each other's funerals and weddings, which cannot of course be regimented into any rigid time-table, and although they have traditionally helped to build each other's houses, an emphasis upon short-term equal exchange has marked a great deal of customary mutual aid between them. It can be argued also in this context that this relatively short-term quality of neighbourhood ties has been to some extent protected by the tendencies to village 'exogamy' mentioned earlier, which helps to prevent the widespread development of kinship ties and concomitant customarily longer-term commitments between neighbours.

All this is highly consonant with the sort of population mobility which I have described for the pre-1974 period and with the related fact that villages at that time were in a variety of interlocking ways both temporal and relatively temporary units. We have seen that a range of factors, both sociological and ecological, have combined to generate and foster the processes in question; and it is perhaps worthwhile to note explicitly here that the factors concerned were operative not only at the village level itself, as we have seen in this section, but also at wider (e.g. chiefdom) and narrower (e.g. household) levels. It may also be remarked that such fluid Nyamwezi settlements contrast systematically with the more or less permanent and closed villages of parts of south Asia and Madagascar (cf. Leach, 1961 and Bloch, 1971) which exhibit, at least ideally, a strong and durable link between a limited area of land and a corporate community, and which are themselves considerably closer to the new villages which the Tanzanian Government has been attempting to establish. It is not surprising in this context that one of my Nyamwezi friends told me that he was less worried about joining one of the *ujamaa* villages in the area than he was about the question of how easily he might be able to get out of it with his wealth intact once he had joined.

I have mentioned that the intensity of customary co-operation between neighbours seems to have diminished in the Kahama area where previously it was very strong. One field of activity which has been involved here is in fact housebuilding from which, as we have seen, the very word for neighbours has been drawn. This is of course an area where the person helped may well derive considerable material benefit, and some problems about this were already beginning to be seen by 1960.

I had some personal experience of such problems which may be worth recounting here, though the details of the case are of course rather special. In 1959 I asked my neighbours if they would be willing to build a house for me, since my tent was reaching the end of its useful life, and they agreed to do so, in their capacity as neighbours, with materials including sisal poles, thatch and mud-bricks which I purchased. In accordance with local custom no payment was given for the labour but the workers were fed with meat provided by me and staple food from my own and their several households.

The house was built within the fields of a Roman Catholic catechist whose recently deceased father had originally agreed to let me pitch my tent there when I first arrived. When I came to leave the area in 1960 I was informed by the catechist that his local priest in nearby Ngaya expected me to give the house to the Church. I mentioned this to the local chief who became quite angry since the field, he claimed, had been allotted to the catechist as an individual rather than by virtue of his office, so that the Church had no claim at all over the land which he saw as a main base of his authority. He cunningly suggested therefore that I follow a recent Native Authority ruling which permitted people to sell their house in cases where they had incurred financial outlay, e.g. on materials, in the building of it. If the Church bought the house, they could use it, though they would be buying it and not the land. If others bought it they could pull it down and make use of the thatch and timbers elsewhere.

When my neighbours heard of all this, they too significantly had their complaints. They had built the house, they said, and it was theirs much more than the Church's. Moreover, very few of them were Christians of any denomination. In the end, all parties concerned except, initially, the Church were satisfied when I sold the house to a man from a neighbouring village for a bull and a sheep which I used to feast my neighbours and friends before leaving the field. Ultimately, I learned later, the Church bought the house from this other man and used it for prayers until it began to fall into decay.

It seems clear that traditionally the fact that a man might move

73

away after his house had been built for him by his neighbours was mitigated by a number of considerations. Firstly, village houses could not legally be sold before the ruling I have mentioned, and most houses in the area did not in any case last more than ten to fifteen years. A newcomer to a village might thus move without charge into a previous villager's house and would know that in doing so he was 'inheriting' an obligation to help others with their building work and might well need their renewed assistance in the future. The ruling about selling, and the reasons behind it, rather ran against the grain of this, however. For it was designed not only to allow a person to offset his outlay on materials, as in my case, but also to provide some compensation for the growing number of people who were beginning to hire expert help in the course of housebuilding; and this development within the building process had a variety of implications including a tendency to greater variation in the quality of local housing. Thus, while many people still had mud and wattle huts with thatched roofs and makeshift doors, others were beginning to build slightly more elaborate dwellings with craftsman-made wooden doors and window frames and corrugated iron roofs, all of which tended both to limit and devalue the amount of physical help given by neighbours. In view of all this, it was not altogether surprising that I found that relatively little mutual aid in housebuilding was taking place in the Busangi area in 1974–5 as compared with 1959; and it may be added here that the Government's encouragement of people to build higher quality and more durable housing for themselves in their new villages seems likely to diminish such co-operation even further.

Two other fields in which I found that neighbourhood collaboration had decreased in the post-Independence years were millet-threshing and informal court hearings. The decline in threshing-team activity, which had been of great importance as a local-level social base for TANU's Independence struggle in the area (Abrahams, 1965 and 1967a), was naturally enough closely linked to the fall in popularity of bulrush millet as a staple crop which I referred to in Chapter 1. This was not, however, the only factor involved, for it appears that there was also some development of the use by individuals of hired lorries for doing threshing work. This practice had been resisted in the politically sensitive climate of the late 1950s as a threat to neighbourhood solidarity, and the resistance seems to have grown weaker once Independence had been achieved and the oppositional political functions of neighbourhood had in consequence lost much of their force.

I have already discussed the problems which began to surround neighbourhood court hearings in the period in question. Here I need only reiterate that the deeply engrained idea of a relatively autonomous field of local community 'political' activity outside the national framework seems no more popular with Tanzania's modern Government and Party than it was with their colonial predecessors; and any contemporary opposition between the community and the Government certainly lacks the justification which the freedom struggles of the 1950s provided. Some possibilities for accommodation of 'elders" tribunals within the national framework does exist, as I have mentioned, but there is still uncertainty about its exact nature and it seems unlikely that the powers of such gatherings to fine offenders will ever be officially recognised.

Modern developments:
from local custom to party policy

The customary collaboration between neighbours which I have discussed has more or less by definition been their own grass-roots creation, and it is perhaps unfortunate that such collaboration has decreased at just the time the Tanzanian Government has expressed the wish to build on its and similar foundations. In the case of neighbourhood court hearings, we have of course seen that these have been affected by other areas of Government policy, and this reflects a broader tension between the desire to unify administratively and ideologically and the desire to make use of and encourage political creativity and a good degree of self-determination at the local level. On the other hand it can be argued that the trends away from mutual aid in housebuilding and agriculture represent, to some extent at least, part of the problems in the country as a whole to which President Nyerere was referring in the passage quoted earlier (see p. 54), and that as such they help to justify the Government's increasing concern with and intervention in the organisation of village life. The situation is, moreover, further complicated by the fact that customary patterns of co-operation, as I have described, appear to assume and cater for less stable villages and village populations than the Government itself finds desirable.

I have already mentioned in a variety of contexts the large-scale movement of the population into new villages since 1974 and the incorporation of these into the framework of the 1975 Village and

Ujamaa Village Registration Act. The new villages are nucleated settlements with a central residential area around which lie the main village fields quite often at considerable walking distance away. The basic common plan of residence in all these settlements is their division into one-acre house-and-garden plots each occupied by a single household. These plots are arranged, when it is feasible to do so, into blocks of two adjacent rows of five which are designed to provide the residential base for ten-house Party cells. The blocks are divided from each other by wide, earthen 'streets' which need to be kept clear of weeds. Ideally there should be between 250 and 600 plots per village. Each plot is normally held by a married couple and their young children or by a single able-bodied adult, and the old and infirm typically live with an adult child or other able-bodied person. It is hoped that each plot-holder will build a relatively permanent house, for example out of concrete building blocks and with a corrugated iron roof.

The new villages are seen as furnishing the basis for the development of a materially and socially improved way of life for their inhabitants. Materially it is argued that nucleated communities can be much more easily provided with good local educational and medical services and ultimately with supplies of running water, though this last still seems to be a long way off for many villages. It is also expected that they will be agriculturally more productive than their predecessors. At least some individual holdings have now been organised on a block farm basis in many villages, and it is hoped that this will make for better use of fertiliser, pesticides, selected seeds, and (in suitable cases) tractors, than was possible with more scattered settlements. Payment for these and the planning of their use is organised through the new Village Co-operative structure in each new village, as is the marketing of cash crops. Under this new system each village *is* a Co-operative in which every adult member of the village is involved, whereas in the past Co-operative and village organisation did not coincide and Co-operative membership was not compulsory.

Socially, it has been hoped, as I have explained, that the movement of people into these new villages will be a first step towards the goal of full-fledged *ujamaa*. Even before this final stage is reached, however, it is officially envisaged that the villages should be socially and politically more desirable places to live. Every villager over 18 years of age is an enfranchised member of the village and has a right to participate to some degree in the organisation of the community's affairs. As will be clear from the previous chapter, Party members now have a right to take part in all levels of village decision-making, but even those who are not members of the Party can express their views at Village Assemblies and some of them may also perhaps play a fuller role than this in various village, as opposed to simply Party-branch, activities. Thus, there is an elected Village Council which has a variety of committees attached to it, and some of these have sub-committees under them. The Party Branch Chairman and Secretary are Chairman and Secretary respectively of the Village Council, but twenty-three members are also elected at least potentially from among all the village members who are over 21 years of age. The Council's Committees normally have five Council members each (some individuals sit on more than one Committee), and up to two non-voting co-opted members. The committees are as follows:

1 Planning and Finance Committee
2 Production and Marketing Committee
3 Education, Culture and Welfare Committee
4 Safety and Security Committee
5 Building and Transport Committee

The Council's functions are officially laid down in the 1975 Act as being,

a to do all such acts and things as are necessary or expedient for the economic and social development of the village,
b to initiate and undertake any task, venture or enterprise as is designed to ensure the welfare and well-being of the residents of the village,
c to plan and co-ordinate the activities of and render assistance and advice to the residents of the village engaged in agricultural, horticultural, forestry or other activity or industry whatsoever,
d to encourage the residents of the village in undertaking and participating in communal enterprises,
e to participate, by way of partnership or otherwise, in economic enterprises with other Village Councils.

The work of the Councils' Committees has been set out in the previously mentioned guidebook to the 1975 Act which was published in the same year by the Prime Minister's Office. In most cases the Committee's titles are themselves more or less self-explanatory for present purposes but the following points may be noted. The Planning and

Finance Committee's duties include the allocation of land for different purposes including individual use and it may have under it a sub-committee for organising a village shop and a sub-committee for Investment and Loans. The Safety and Security Committee's functions include the organisation of the Peoples' Militia (*Jeshi la Mgambo*) which all able-bodied persons over 18 years of age should be involved in. The militia's training sessions are designed to toughen people physically and to heighten their political awareness. The Building and Transport Committee is expected not only to engage in public building works but also to encourage people to build better quality housing for themselves in the village. It is also charged with monitoring villagers' travel arrangements.

The comments I made in the previous chapter concerning the opportunities which Party arrangements provide for villagers to play a more energetic role in the organisation of their own lives are further highlighted by the data I have just presented on the wider administrative structure of new villages. At least in theory, the opportunities both within and outside the Party organisation seem to be substantial and a failure to try to take advantage of them renders discontented villagers somewhat vulnerable to criticism. At the same time one must recognise, however, that the reality is not quite so straightforward. Thus, I am told, it is rather hard in practice for non-Party members to move into responsible positions in many villages; and even granting a partial solution of this problem through increased party membership, it seems clear that some factors will still tend at least to inhibit genuine political expression by many villagers. For people are, if nothing else, anxious to avoid making life difficult for themselves by being branded as 'trouble makers' and 'disloyal' by the authorities above them. This applies in varying degrees in different villages both to the case of ordinary villagers in their relations with more entrenched elements in the village party structure, and also to the external relations between villagers (including party officials) and those in authority at higher levels of the system when their interests fail to coincide.

However this political issue is eventually resolved, there are also a number of other factors which are worth noting here as likely to affect the viability of these new experimental forms of village. In the short to medium term the success or failure of Government to fulfil the promises of better local health and social services is likely to affect morale, though the financial and organisational problems of the recent war effort against Uganda may possibly provide a popularly acceptable if brief respite on this domestic front. Similarly the relative success of block farm and other new agricultural developments is going to be important. Results in the Nyamwezi area so far appear to have been mixed and it is possible that fluctuations in annual rainfall will make an authoritative assessment of progress very difficult until several years have passed. It must be said in this context, however, that the arrangement whereby villagers now live near to actual or projected social services and at much greater distance from their fields than in the past has been a source of considerable dissatisfaction which even good services and large increases in output will not easily remove. The inconvenience of this was spelled out to me on more than one occasion. Some people stressed the simple fact that they did not like to walk regularly so far to work in the fields, and that they would prefer to walk some way occasionally to a dispensary. They also pointed out that it was hard at a distance to keep pests off the crops and they did not like to have to transport their harvests a long way back home, a problem which would of course be made worse by increased production. In one case it was pointed out that a woman had to leave her infirm husband on his own at home while she was cultivating, so that she was out of reach if he should briefly need her help or even simply want her company. Some villagers, moreover, feared that the proximity of dwellings in the new compact settlements would be a health and fire hazard which would require better medical facilities by their very nature, and this fear merged also into worries about witchcraft which I touch on later. It also appears likely that compact settlement will create difficulties in areas where many householders keep large herds of cattle. In Busangi village there were not many such men, and they were mainly living on plots on the edge of the village which enabled them to move their cows about without undue disturbance to their neighbours' homes and gardens. This would be more difficult with larger numbers and could easily lead to conflict in a crowded area.

It is possible that some alleviation of the difficulties of compact settlement may be found in the planned or simply *de facto* development of more complex residential patterns in which people might, for example, move out temporarily to huts near their fields during the agricultural season. Indeed, I understand that such arrangements are beginning to emerge in a few areas at the time of writing, and that some larger villages are already developing slightly more dispersed structures in which a number of compact 'satellite' hamlets (*vitongoji*) are clustered loosely round a central zone. There is a danger, however, that such compromises may bring the worst of both worlds rather than the best to those adopting them. The quality of seasonal housing near to fields is likely to be worse than that of permanent dwellings, and people in such accommodation will be most distant from social services during the rains and the period of hardest work when travel is most inconvenient and much sickness occurs. Again, the 'satellite' arrangement I have mentioned may bring people rather nearer to their fields and permit more flexibility of cattle movement, but it will still have the disadvantages which villagers perceive in compact settlement, while removing them from the immediate access to all central facilities which was a major aim of villagisation.

There are also a number of longer-term issues which will have to be successfully resolved, and the nature of these has already been outlined in my account of pre-1974 settlement patterns. A main ecological problem will undoubtedly be that of maintaining the longer-term fertility of the soils within and surrounding the new villages. In some cases, where villages have been sited in newly opened areas, this is likely to be less difficult than in others, such as Busangi, where the residential part of the village itself has been mainly set up on a rather worn-out area of land (the old village of Kibama) which was conveniently empty only because many people had died or moved away from the site and had not been replaced by newcomers. Moreover, if this question of fertility of land can be dealt with successfully at an economic price which community and country can afford, then serious social structural problems are also likely to emerge.

Thus, it is not yet clear how the new structures, with their emphasis upon the long-term, well-housed occupation of a fixed, well-serviced area, will be able to absorb growing village populations and the demands for extra space and fertile soil created by domestic developmental processes. The planners are clearly aware that there are serious constraints upon the maximum and minimum size of viable communities – they know that it is hard to provide adequate services and land within reach for a group that is too large and it is not economic to supply the services and facilities concerned to a village which is very small. This last point, however, means that the traditional processes whereby large flourishing communities gradually and 'naturally' grew up from small pioneer beginnings, often in initially remote but fertile places, are no longer possible under the new arrangements. It remains to be seen what alternative strategies will emerge in these new circumstances. Before going further, however, it may be worthwhile noting here that the earlier mentioned preference for 'hoe' over 'house' symbol candidates in the parliamentary elections (see Chapter 2) fits remarkably well with the people's own indigenous solutions to problems of this sort. For it can be argued that their choice of 'hoe candidates' reflects not simply their strong interest in agriculture but also their awareness of the possibility of contradiction between successful enterprise in this field and static residential patterns. Hoe and house were officially chosen originally as a pair of positively valued symbols which should each equally appeal to everyone. The fact that they might seriously conflict was not apparently envisaged, and it is not perhaps too fanciful to suggest that a closer look at voting behaviour in this context might usefully have engendered greater caution in the drafting and implementation of the 1974–5 villagisation scheme.

If the villages do in fact manage to become established as relatively permanent communities with a substantially slower or at least more staggered and more organised pattern of population movement than existed up to 1974, it appears likely that they will also need to resolve a variety of existing conflicts arising out of divorce, polygyny and infant mortality, and that they will in addition face some new strains in the field of customary co-operation between kin and affines who live in different villages. I will say a little more about this last point in the next section and chapter, but it may be recalled more generally here that many of the existing conflicts concerned are typically expressed in terms of fears and accusations about sickness and witchcraft which were partly handled in the past through the highly valued possibility of relatively unrestricted movement to another area. One Divisional Secretary I spoke to about this responded blandly that better medical facilities would help quell anxieties of this sort. Another, perhaps significantly a Sukuma who was used to similar problems in his home area, told me that he was sure that witchcraft fears and accusations would increase in the new villages and he proposed, how seriously I am not sure, that the solution might in due course have to be the establishment of 'villages of witches' whose members would be those identified as such in other communities.

Overall it seems clear that the social system of the early 1970s will be subjected to, and will at the same time generate, considerable stress in this new relatively bounded environment. I write of it as bounded in this context because of the attempt to make each village community a distinct and continuingly viable entity in its own right, but it is of

81

course equally true that the new villages have been established on a common basis as a direct result of their ever deepening involvement in the nation. This raises one last point in this section, that the villages of Unyamwezi are now substantially dependent for their continued existence, as for their creation, on the maintenance of relevant trends of policy at the national level. As such one may note that their future fate may be determined as much by the pressures from other parts of Tanzania and from outside to which that policy is exposed as by the internal relatively local-level dynamics whose main forces I have tried here to delineate.

Ujamaa in Unyamwezi

As I have described, it is a stated aim of the new system that villages should ideally develop in due course into officially recognised *ujamaa* communities. These are expected to be characterised by strong sentiments of mutual responsibility and a firm commitment to socialism and the 1975 Villages Act specifies that a 'substantial portion of the economic activites of the village' must be 'undertaken and carried out on a communal basis' before a recommendation for its official recognition can be made. Such communal organisation in different parts of Tanzania has typically involved the existence of village fields which have been jointly cultivated, and the proceeds from the sale of crops has subsequently been distributed according to the labour input of the village members. Other enterprises such as communally owned shops and flour mills have also been quite common. In all cases income is distributed after payment of the group's expenses and, ideally, after money has been paid into the Village's Reserve Fund which is used to help to pay for projects and also to provide security against a 'rainy day' or, in this area, more usually a dry one.

Some such communities were of course already in existence in the Nyamwezi area in 1974–5 and their special nature merits some attention here, even though not many people were involved in them. As the earlier mentioned President's Report suggests, the people of this area have not been generally responsive to the call to *ujamaa*. I do not have exact figures for Tabora Region but they do not seem likely to have differed seriously from the figure of under 3 per cent membership quoted for Shinyanga Region, and the detailed figures which I have for Kahama District show even 3 per cent to be a relatively high point of reference. Thus in August 1973 the District contained 31 such villages which had a total population of 2,215 men, women and children, or

82

approximately 1¼ per cent of the estimated total population of the District at that time. By December 1974 the number of such villages had decreased to 20 but the listed population in them had in fact increased to 3,314. The fall in the number of villages was due to a variety of factors which included the failure of some of them to function successfully, and the 1974 'operations' themselves provided a stimulus to disband some of these. At the same time, the same programme of resettlement was the most important single factor in the increase in the total number of *ujamaa* villagers. For many people joined in order to avoid being moved into brand new settlements when they gathered that successful *ujamaa* villages were much less likely to be made to move. Many moreover suspected, incorrectly it appears, that an early enforcement of *ujamaa* organisation would follow the resettlements in any case.

The artificial rise in the population of these villages was verified for me by one of the officials at the District level, and he pointed out that it did not bode well for their future viability. He also corroborated what I had previously heard from unofficial sources that a number of the less successful villages had simply been started by individuals whose motives were not wholly in accord with the ideals of the system. Some ambitious politicians had tried to attract people to join them in such schemes in order to enhance their careers through success as *ujamaa* leaders, and although such ambition was by no means necessarily unproductive or, indeed, totally illegitimate, its fading for reasons which had nothing to do with village organisation as such had occasionally led to the collapse of villages. Thus in one case a village leader had lost interest in the community once he had managed to be elected to Parliament, though it was said that he would no doubt try to get it going again if he stood for re-election. Such men offered various enticements to people, such as the likelihood of access to special financial and other aid which early *ujamaa* villages were often given, and this prospect seems to have attracted many to the villages in the early years. Thus the *ujamaa* village of Kisuke, which adjoined the new development village of that name, had seventeen household heads in 1974–5, but I was told by the Chairman of the village that there had been almost a hundred of them when the village started in 1969. The majority of these, he told me scornfully, had come expecting an aid-subsidised easy life but had been fairly rapidly disillusioned. Similar disappointments about quick and easy profits and, occasionally, problems of mismanagement of funds had led to the complete failure of several villages which lacked the hard core of determined members which Kisuke had.

Despite all this, a number of villages had worked reasonably well in Kahama District and four of them, including Kisuke, were well known as more successful enterprises. The others were Vumilia, Wame and Ulowa I and I will say a little about these and Kisuke. Of the four, I know least in detail about Vumilia and most about Kisuke where I stayed for several days.

Vumilia (the name is a Swahili word which means 'persevere') was a rather special case and one about which some officials seemed to have mixed feelings. It was situated near Kahama Town and, unlike most other villages, it obtained a large part of its corporate income not from agriculture – there were only 3 acres of maize and 7 acres of cotton under communal control – but from the brewing and the sale of beer. It was moreover mainly a women's community. For, whereas the sex ratio in most other villages was fairly evenly balanced and some even had a preponderance of men, Vumilia had 56 adult women members and only 18 men in 1974. The combination of relatively independent womanhood and beer brewing is not uncommon in itself in the area, but it was unusual as the basis of a whole community and it was clearly not a type of village which officials wished to see developed in large numbers in the area. Nonetheless it was agreed to be a rather profitable enterprise. I do not unfortunately have details of their total income in a year, but it appears that in August 1973 the community had a reserve fund of 34,000 Tanzanian shillings and this had risen to 43,000 shillings by the following year.

Ulowa I was part of a tobacco-growing scheme in the south of Kahama District. The scheme contained six villages (Ulowa I–VI) and two of these (Ulowa I & V) were registered as *ujamaa* communities. The other four villages were organised simply on a basis of individual household production. The village was started about 1970 with five communally-held acres of tobacco which yielded 13,300 shillings after expenses. By December 1974 it had 75 men and 78 women members and a total population of 330 including children and old people. I was told that a large number of the 153 adults were relatively young and that this was owing to the fact that the work was very hard. Twenty-two acres of tobacco were under communal cultivation, and the villagers had also planted some 42 acres of maize in a communal field. Income was derived from selling these crops and from the community's possession of a flour mill which they ran commercially. The villagers' joint income was 43,438 shillings in 1973–4, which averages a little under 300 shillings per adult person and around 600 shillings per married couple. People were paid a share on the basis of the labour days they had contributed, and their income from this will have been supplemented in many cases by profits from the sale of produce grown on private holdings. It is some indication of the general situation that this village was one of the most profitable *ujamaa* communities in the District. It seems likely that tobacco is a relatively suitable crop for joint production since it can benefit from co-operative work in the preparation of seed beds and in the organisation of drying, which has to be carefully monitored on a day- and night-shift basis. The provision of communal drying sheds and storage facilities is also a help.

In spite of the advantages of growing both a profitable and a 'complex' crop, I was informed slightly regretfully by local officials that rather higher individual incomes were often obtained in those other villages of the scheme which were organised in single-family holdings. There, as in many Tabora District villages, small and fairly simple individually-owned drying barns had been constructed and only storage sheds were jointly owned. Each family in these villages individually planted and processed its own tobacco and other crops, and people were paid for the amount they had produced rather than for their labour input. I do not have full details of the income in these other villages but it seems from the limited data at my disposal that the higher incomes concerned are not necessarily evidence of a failure of *ujamaa* to achieve its aims. Firstly, it appears that it was the range of incomes in these villages rather than the average which was mainly different from Ulowa I's, so that while some individuals were earning rather large amounts – figures of 4,000–6,000 shillings were quoted to me – some others were receiving rather less than they might have got out of the more regular communal work patterns of an *ujamaa* community. Secondly, it is very possible that the most successful individual farmers depended on the use of hired labour to grow as much tobacco as they did, and this, though not illegal, at least runs against the grain of official Tanzanian socialist ideals.[4]

The *ujamaa* village of Wame was started in 1970 under the Chairmanship of a local TANU leader, Antoni, who was in fact District Chairman of the Party. Like some other villages, as I have mentioned, Wame was quite small before the 'operations' and contained only about 20 families, but the numbers had increased by mid-January

1975 to 112 men and 132 women and their children. Villagers were supposed to work a six-day week on the communal fields during the cultivation season, though time-off was granted for work on individual plots. Income was earned as elsewhere according to the number of days worked, and men and women were paid individually for their work. People who failed to work when required, or who broke other rules of co-operation, were warned first and could be fined and even expelled from the village if they failed to heed the warnings. The fines were basically the same as the *masumule* charged traditionally in villages in the area for offences against the rules of neighbourhood co-operation. People cultivated in teams to songs and the beat of drums, and the work of song leaders and drummers was paid for in the same way as cultivation. I do not have figures on the income of the village from its communal fields, but the acreage under cultivation (50 acres of cotton and 76 acres of maize) was rather large by local standards and the village was in fact judged as the best *ujamaa* village in Shinyanga Region for 1975. Even so, it may be noted that the villagers cultivated privately a total of some 238 acres and their communal fields, though large and impressive to the eye, amounted to less than one quarter acre of cotton and under a third of an acre of maize per adult member.

Kisuke was a small village some 40 kilometres south of Kahama Town. A development village had been started next to it in 1974 and people had lived nearby before then, but it had kept its numbers low after the initial influx which I have referred to earlier. When I visited the village in 1975 it contained sixteen married men, most of their wives, and one unmarried woman. One or two wives were due to be enrolled shortly and it may be noted that it is not allowed normally for a polygynous man to have one wife in one village and another in a second and possibly non-*ujamaa* community. The work-plan for the village involved five days of work on communal activities including agriculture, and the weekends were free for individuals to cultivate their own crops. When I stayed in the village in late January, the people had some 30 acres of maize under joint cultivation and 4 acres of cotton. They hoped to extend the maize substantially but could do little more about the unusually low cotton acreage at that stage. Fifteen acres had been planted in previous years and I was told that this year's planting had been delayed through problems of land allocation to newcomers in the neighbouring new 'development village'. As in Wame, communal cultivation was accompanied by drums and songs, and it may be added that this is in the pattern of traditional cultivation team activities in the area. In addition to the communal fields, each wife of a man – and the one unmarried woman – was allocated a one-acre plot for private cultivation. There was in fact a rather high rate of polygyny in the village since two of the 16 men had three wives and a further six had two wives each. Like Ulowa I, the village had a large contingent of younger members, though this appears to be true of relatively new communities in recently opened areas in any case, as I have pointed out. The ages of the sixteen male members of the village are shown in Table 3.3 which also shows the age distribution of polygynists. In addition to these men, and the single woman who was about 50 years of age, the community also contained three old and infirm people who were attached to others' households. It may be noted that eleven of the household heads were Nyamwezi and six were Sumbwa. There were three pairs of full brothers in the village and there was also a classificatory 'sister's son' of the Chairman and a classificatory 'son' of the single woman.

Table 3.3: Male members of Kisuke *ujamaa* village (age and polygyny), 1975

Age	Number	Polygynous
20–29	5	2
30–39	5	4
40–49	4	1
50–54	1	–
55–59	1	1

In addition to its fields, the village also owned a communal shop, and it had been provided with a piped water supply, which was temporarily out of action, and a school which was also attended by children from neigbouring settlements. There were two other shops and also a flour mill which were privately owned.

The affairs of the village were run by an elected committee of ten members headed by the Chairman. He was about 45 years old and was a founding member of the village. He had been one of the first to clear land in the area in the early 1960s. The Chairman was aided by a Secretary and a Treasurer who were also founding members of the village. The Secretary was in his late twenties but he also belonged to a family who had cleared land in the vicinity. The Treasurer was about 45 years of age and had come into the area to clear land in 1963. Five other members of the village had been founding members, and there had in fact been only seven families after the first bubble of enthusiasm burst, and numbers had then gradually increased to those I found there.

The villagers' income from *ujamaa* activity was reported as a little over 350 shillings per head on average in 1973–4, but it is possible that this figure should have been higher since the Police began to investigate an apparent irregularity in the village accounts early in 1975. I was told by the Chairman that a sum of over 6,000 shillings was possibly involved and that the problem lay with amounts charged to expenses. I do not have details of the outcome of these investigations. Cases of mismanagement or misappropriation of communal funds were fairly well known and were a source of some anxiety, which was sometimes justified and sometimes not. It should perhaps be said here that Kisuke villagers in general exhibited an impressive determination to combine prosperity with a commitment to mutual responsibility and aid, and some of the younger more recent members expressed a particularly strong attachment to President Nyerere's ideals.

Since wives were also usually members of the village, the total income of a family out of *ujamaa* activities tended to be somewhat larger than the figure of just over 350 shillings I have mentioned. Each individual member, however, received his or her own portion of the village income, and in theory at least a wife's income was her own. I was told that how she used it, e.g. for herself or as a contribution to the household budget, was typically a matter of agreement between her and her husband. This seems to be the case in other such villages also. Even when wives put their income in a common household fund, however, I gathered they were rather more independent financially than women in the normal run of Nyamwezi villages. *Ujamaa* thus appears to have been a potential source, though not a strong one, of change in the status of women and relations between them and their husbands. Another possible area of change appeared to be in relations between *ujamaa* villagers and their kin and affines outside the village. Members needed to ask permission to leave the village temporarily to help such people, for example in their agricultural work, and this tended to inhibit interpersonal co-operation across village boundaries. So far, the problem seems to have been very small but it is worth monitoring for the future since such co-operation is important for the maintenance of the ties in question.

It will be clear from my account that *ujamaa* was by no means flourishing in Unyamwezi in the period under discussion. Not many people were involved and not many of the villages were particularly successful enterprises. Even in the more successful villages, moreover, the actual amount of *ujamaa* activity, as measured in the communal acreages under cultivation for example, was not especially great and incomes were not very high. This, however, must be measured in all fairness against the relatively low average incomes of cultivators in non-*ujamaa* communities and against the low as well as the high end of the range of such incomes. It is beyond the scope of the data I possess to give detailed figures on this, but the point made about Ulowa I, that incomes there may have tended to be closer to the average than in non-*ujamaa* villages in the complex, probably applies also elsewhere. Certainly it would be wrong to imply that *ujamaa* villagers were in general either the rich or the poor of Unyamwezi.

The movement of people into new villages, which was hoped to lead to the eventual development of *ujamaa*, has in the short run actually had the opposite effect. Most of the pre-existent *ujamaa* villages were very small and they do not appear to have grown sufficiently, even with a pre-'operations' influx of new members, to qualify as registered villages under the new Act. A registered village should normally have a minimum of 250 households – the word *kaya* which is found in Kinyamwezi and some other Bantu languages is officially used for these households – and I understand that villages such as Kisukc and Wame have now been joined with other groups to constitute simply new 'registered villages' which have not yet developed sufficient overall communal enterprise to be formally designated *ujamaa* communities. At present, then, there are at most a very few if any *ujamaa* villages in the Nyamwezi area – I have in fact not found any formally announced in the Government's official *Gazeti* (Gazette) up to early 1979 – and it is as yet unclear whether the communal spirit which moved small numbers in the past to establish the pre-1975 *ujamaa* villages can be generated in the future on the larger scale demanded by the new village system.

4 Marriage and kinship

The various homesteads and households (*kaya*) which combine for longer or shorter periods to form a Nyamwezi village usually have male heads who are married, and it may be said in general that marriage has been the core institution of Nyamwezi social and economic organisation at the domestic level. Husband and wife are typically the central members of a domestic group, forming an economic team which works together along the lines of a well-developed complementary division of labour to produce a large part of their joint subsistence needs. At its simplest, a household will begin with a young married couple who will live and work together and have children who will themselves eventually marry and establish households of their own. This simple pattern is, however, often subject to considerable modification in reality. Firstly, it is complicated by at least a male ideal of polygyny which itself is only partly realised, and there is the further fact that divorce is rather common in the area. In addition, different forms of marriage occur with different customary implications for rights over children and their residence, and the situation is further complicated by the modern system of magistrates' courts described in Chapter 2.

I begin my discussion with an account of the main forms of marriage, and I then examine their distribution, and the incidence of divorce and polygyny. An analysis of the functions of marriage and the related features of household and domestic groups, with their well-developed division of labour between the sexes, is followed by a discussion of the structure of the Nyamwezi kinship system. As with marriage, a major feature of this system has traditionally been an emphasis upon the difference between the sexes, with a tendency towards male domination in a wide variety of contexts. In the final section I discuss some of the emerging forces for change, which may slowly be beginning to push this and other features of Nyamwezi kinship and marriage into new forms and directions.

The main forms of marriage

An account of the main forms of marriage in the area will be useful at this point. The existence there of a wide range of marriage custom has been noted by many writers – one mentions five named types of marriage – and it is clear that new forms have emerged from time to time while others have become less popular. Many of the features which distinguish one type from another consist of variations in the details or elaboration of the customary procedure at the different stages of a marriage, and such variation is perhaps to be expected in domestic custom in an area with a diverse and mobile population in which some individuals are, by local standards, rather better off than others.

When they are looked at from the viewpoint of their jural consequences, the several types of marriage are fairly readily reduced to two main classes – marriage with and marriage without bridewealth – and it is perhaps worth stressing that, despite the differences between them, even these have much in common. Thus adultery is recognised as an offence in either case, though the penalties are not identical; and either form can be converted into the other, though the conversion from a bridewealth to a non-bridewealth union is an exceptional occurrence. The verb *kutola* and its passive form *kutolwa*, which are the standard words for 'marrying', are moreover used to describe, respectively, a man's and a woman's entry into either form of union and, more generally, it may be noted that a woman's residence in the homestead of a man, her engagement in its economic activities and her cooking for and sleeping with him are together usually sufficient grounds within the Nyamwezi frame of reference to consider her to be his wife (*nke*). It may be added that the inclusion of a sexual component in such a relationship customarily marks it off from one between kin – for some men temporarily reside and collaborate with a mother or a sister – since, with the exception of some Sumbwa who may marry certain cousins, sexual relations between known kin are normally prohibited in the area; and while breaches of this rule may occasionally be condoned when the relationship is a more distant one, this is by no means automatic.

Non-bridewealth marriages commonly begin with an elopement at night, the man sometimes leaving a small token on the woman's bed. The woman's father or other guardian may then try to obtain bridewealth from the man, and this is most likely – and most likely to succeed – in the case of a previously unmarried girl. In some parts of the region the man may also have to pay a penalty of one cow to the woman's guardian, even if he does not go on to pay bridewealth for

91

her. Such payments, called *mchenya*, have become quite common in the northern Nyamwezi area in recent years and are probably connected with the modern development there of profitable cash-cropping with a subsequent increment in the 'cash' value of a woman's labour. A man should also pay at least a few shillings to his new wife when he first brings her home, especially if there is anyone there, such as his father, who will be a senior male 'in-law' to her. Without at least a promise of this payment, which is called *bugila* and is also due in bridewealth marriage, a woman should not eat in the man's homestead.

A non-bridewealth wife should – like her bridewealth counterpart – be given the wherewithal for the establishment of her own household. Mainly this consists of fields, seed and her own hut with its separate cooking hearth, and the provision of these should be arranged by her husband or his senior kin at the earliest reasonable opportunity. She also has the right to her husband's support and participation in agricultural and other household activities and she is entitled to expect him to sleep regularly with her. The husband in turn has similar rights to his wife's labour and sexual services, but he also has a non-reciprocated right to her fidelity and he may take an adulterer to court. Such an adulterer can be fined, but customarily no compensation is awarded to a husband who has not paid bridewealth and he has no rights to any offspring of his wife's adultery. On the ritual side, he can consult a diviner for himself about his wife's health and well-being but, unlike the husband in a bridewealth marriage, he is not entitled to accompany her kin if they make such a consultation.

Unless redemption payments have been made for them, the children of a non-bridewealth marriage belong in Nyamwezi customary law to the wife's kin, who are entitled to take custody of them when they reach about 8 years of age. Maternal kin, however, may sometimes forgo this right, especially in the case of daughters whom they may prefer to allow to remain with and help their mother. The father of such children has no right to receive the bridewealth from his daughters' marriages and no right or obligation to pay bridewealth for his sons. These are their maternal kin's affairs. Such children also have no right to inherit any property left by their father unless other more eligible kin are absent or choose to share it with them.

Despite all this, a father is by no means wholly without rights and responsibilities *vis-à-vis* such children. He should support them as youngsters while they are living with him and he is responsible for their behaviour at that time. Most importantly, he also has the clearly acknowledged right to make redemption payments to his wife's kin for them, either in childhood or later, and it is even possible for a father to redeem his daughter shortly after bridewealth has been paid for her, and to receive the considerable difference between the bridewealth and the payments needed to redeem her.

The basic customary payments to redeem a child are two cows and a bull, or their equivalent in cash or smallstock, for a daughter; and one cow and a bull or their equivalent for a son. The people explain this difference in terms of a girl's potential as a source of bridewealth and a bearer of children, and also in terms of the value of her domestic and agricultural labour. According to local customary evaluations, the difference between a daughter and a son in this respect is not quite as great as that between a cow and a bull (one cow equals two bulls) but it is not far off. In addition to these basic payments, a father may also have to pay a sum called *lulelelo* (literally 'for rearing') in recognition of the contribution which maternal kin have made to bringing up the child, and he may also be asked to pay off any debts outstanding for *bugila*. In the case of a first child he should make a further payment, called *masani*, which consists of two cloths or their cash equivalent for the wife's mother. This is also paid in bridewealth marriages as part of the bridewealth itself.

The word used for redeeming children, the transitive verb *kukwa*, is also the most general term for marrying a wife with bridewealth. This suggests, correctly, that bridewealth itself is intimately connected with rights over children.[1] There are, however, a few differences between the two forms of payment. Whereas bridewealth covers all the offspring of a marriage, redemption involves separate payments for each child and the total paid may be more or less than bridewealth would have been, depending largely on the number of the children. Payments to redeem a child are, moreover, not in any way returnable upon divorce if the child should happen to have died, whereas account is taken of such a death if bridewealth is returned.

Traditionally, the wife in a non-bridewealth marriage was, like her bridewealth counterpart, only entitled to take with her on divorce the property with which she came and any proceeds of a craft, such as pottery, in which she might be skilled. By the 1950s, however, it had become customary for such a wife to claim half of any produce of which she had been the co-producer with her husband, and this in part reflected the development of greater opportunities for men to exploit women economically in such unions. Similar claims were not permitted in the case of wives in bridewealth marriages since the right to their labour had been 'paid for', and such marriages could not be entered and dissolved quite so easily at a man's convenience.

According to some older people, the transformation of a non-bridewealth marriage into a bridewealth one used in their younger days to involve the making of a set of named payments which marked the assumption by the man of a full complement of rights and obligations as husband and father.[2] Similarly patterns are occasionally found today but actual practice varies from one marriage to another and, in fact, seems likely always to have done so. Sometimes a girl's guardian may simply demand or be offered a lump sum which will be understood to cover the full costs of the transformation. Sometimes some named payments are demanded while others are not. It appears that often such named demands are used at least as much in order to ensure that a reasonably large sum is paid, as to guarantee that all the different aspects of the transaction are covered. Certainly, by no means everyone is clear about the exact significance of some named payments.

The conversion of a non-bridewealth to a bridewealth marriage usually takes place, if at all, during the first few years of the union, and it may well in fact be resisted by the wife's kin if it is attempted at a later stage, especially if the couple have had many children, whom it would cost more to redeem individually. Such early conversion of non-bridewealth unions tends to some extent to blur the distinction between them and their bridewealth counterparts since it suggests the possibility that some of them at least may best be seen as a preliminary stage of one or other form of bridewealth marriage. Although the overall situation is more complex, there is a degree of truth in this suggestion, especially in the case of forms of bridewealth marriage known locally as *butwinija* and also sometimes interestingly referred to, like non-bridewealth unions, as *wibozi* or *kubola*. These marriages differ from the most prestigious forms of bridewealth marriage called *winga wa limi* (literally 'daylight wedding') both in their procedure and in the related fact that they are typically cheaper to complete. The use of the related terms *wibozi* and *kubola* for these marriages appears to derive from the fact that they typically commence with an elopement even though there is every intention to pay bridewealth more or less at once. Such elopement tends to have the effect of strengthening the hand of the man's side in the subsequent bridewealth negotiations because of the element of *fait accompli* in the situ-

Counting the monetary part of a successfully negotiated bridewealth in a *butwinija* marriage.

A mother blesses the cattle paid for her daughter in the same marriage. She is blowing a mixture of millet flour and water over them.

ation, which is only partly diminished by the temporary return of the girl to her kin in some cases.

Bridewealth negotiations in a *butwinija* marriage are rarely protracted, and marrying in this fashion is more generally a relatively simple affair which lacks many of the elaborate formalities of feasting and ceremonial which mark a full 'daylight wedding'. The amount of bridewealth paid in *butwinija* varies but a figure of around ten head of cattle or their equivalent seems to be fairly common.[3] The negotiations usually begin with a discussion between a pair of representatives (*bakombe*) from each side who are always men and typically neighbours of the parties whom they represent. This discussion may be followed by the direct participation of the girl's guardian and either her husband-to-be or, if he is still relatively young, his guardian. After some haggling, which may involve attempts to insist upon a series of named payments (and thus boost the total amount paid, as noted earlier), a figure is agreed and then there may be more negotiations about how much should be paid at once and how much later. A crucial matter for decision here is the stage in the payments at which the bride's guardian will slaughter a goat *ya kulalucha* (literally 'of reddening') and thus formally signify his satisfaction with the marriage as a bridewealth union. There is some disagreement in the area about the extent of the implications of this goat and particularly whether it entails that the bridewealth given is now fully the property and responsibility of the wife's guardian, e.g. in the event of either loss through death or increment through birth among the transferred livestock. Disputes do occasionally arise over this issue, but they are rarely serious unless the marriage has run into other difficulties.

Full 'daylight weddings' – so-called because they should *not* start with an elopement – are, as I have said, elaborate and relatively expensive affairs. They are the most prestigious way of marrying in the area and are most likely to occur on the first marriage of children of relatively well-to-do families. As such they are not particularly common but they are nonetheless considered locally as Nyamwezi marriage *par excellence*. Despite change and simplification over time, modern forms of such weddings do hark back in many ways to traditional procedure and the following account outlines the major stages of this. For convenience the account assumes that the marriage is a first one for the bride and groom who are residing with their respective parents.

(i) *Courtship*. Commonly a father would tell his son to seek out a wife for himself and the son would look for a suitable girl. He then took one or two male companions to visit the girl at her home and discuss the possibility of marriage with her. Usually a number of such visits were necessary before the girl, after consultation with a grandmother or other friendly kinswoman, would agree to the proposal. If the girl refused the suit, courtship usually had to start afresh elsewhere.

(ii) *Bridewealth negotiations.* If the girl agreed, the parents of the couple were informed and, if they considered the match a suitable one, bridewealth negotiations would begin. Two male neighbours of each father acted as their representatives (*bakombe*) and met at the girl's home for negotiations. These acted on instructions from the fathers who did not themselves participate in direct negotiations. Several visits might well be made before agreement could be reached, and negotiations sometimes proved abortive. The amount agreed consisted of a number of named beasts, e.g. *ya kilezu* (literally 'of the beard') for the girl's paternal grandfather, and *ya mamiye* (literally 'of the maternal uncle'), but extra non-specifically named payments were often agreed as well. Most payments were returnable upon divorce subject to deductions for the birth of children, but some were not, e.g. a bull *ya mazi* (literally 'of the girls' house') which was slaughtered and given to the women of the girl's family and the earlier mentioned payment of two cloths called *masani* for the girl's mother (the name refers to the harness which a mother used to use to carry a child on her back). This last could only be returned if no child was born of the marriage.

(iii) *Feasting and bridewealth collection.* When bridewealth had been agreed the girl's father summoned his own kin and neighbours and gave a feast for people on the groom's side. Arrangements for collection of the bridewealth were made and a delegation from the girl's side would visit the groom's home on an appointed day to choose the actual bridewealth cattle or other goods. After this the visitors were feasted by the groom's father and they then returned home with the bridewealth. Both these feasts are known as *ya bukombe* and, as the name suggests, they celebrate the successful outcome of the bridewealth negotiations. At the second feast the time for the main wedding ceremonies was fixed.

(iv) *The wedding.* The main ceremonies took place at the girl's home and lasted about three days. Representatives of both sides attended and they, and even passers-by, were liberally feasted and there was much singing and dancing. The main events of the wedding were the arrival of the groom and his friends, the search for the bride who was hidden in the homestead, a ceremonial meal eaten by the bride and groom, and bestowal on the couple of public blessings and admonitions by their parents and other relations. Afterwards the groom and his companions were given tasks to do by the bride's father. Sexual consummation of the marriage might take place at the time of the wedding itself or a few days later.

(v) *Removal of the bride.* In the past a newly married couple commonly spent up to a year at the bride's home. When the husband eventually removed his wife she was accompanied by many male and female companions who delayed the journey at regular intervals and demanded various small payments *ya nzila* (literally 'of the way'). Further payments including *bugila* were demanded on arrival, and the bride and her companions would be set small domestic tasks which they refused to do without a payment. The most important ceremonial at this juncture was the showing of respect by the bride and some of her female companions to her husband's father and mother in turn. This involved approaching them in line on their knees and offering them food. This was accompanied by a small exchange of gifts.

Although these traditional procedures tend in most respects to serve as a sort of template of ideal practice for modern 'daylight weddings', two major changes from the pattern have been introduced. Thus the first *bukombe* feast has for many years usually been held at the groom's home, and the girl's family only give their feast after the bridewealth has been collected. This change appears to have sprung from a desire to avoid unnecessary outlay by the bride's family if the marriage should be broken off before bridewealth was transferred. It is also no longer customary for the groom to live for a time with his wife's family before taking her home. More generally, however, and in spite of some curtailment of the ceremonial nowadays at the discretion of the parties, it may be noted that *bukombe* feasts are still expected to be given on both sides, and the traditional forms of music and the blessings at the wedding are still customary, as are the main events of the bride's journey to and her reception at the groom's home. Even modern Christian weddings may incorporate most of the ceremonial involved, and at a Pentecostal wedding I attended in 1975 the blessing of the bride and groom by their kin was built into the church service itself. Muslim weddings, which are mainly found in towns and in the rural areas around Tabora, tend to take a rather different form which is related to Swahili coastal and urban patterns elsewhere. Nonetheless they also often incorporate traditional Nyamwezi songs and other features of the ceremonial I have described.

A man's main rights in bridewealth marriage will already have begun to emerge from my discussion. Customarily he has full rights over his wife's children, irrespective of their actual paternity, providing they are born or conceived during the marriage. He receives his daughter's bridewealth and he should try to provide the bridewealth for at least the first marriages of his sons, who should also inherit the bulk of his property when he dies. On his death his kin have a traditional right, which is often left unexercised in practice, to the return of bridewealth, less deductions for children, if the widow is not inherited by his younger brother or other junior kinsman. Such inheritance itself is very rare these days. Bridewealth is also returnable on divorce, again with deductions for children which are calculated generally at the same rates used to pay for their redemption. The husband in a bridewealth marriage can take an adulterer to court and receive compensation from him in addition to any fine that he may pay, though the courts usually place limits on the number of times a man may claim concerning any one particular wife. As I have implied, an adulterer has no customary right to any child born of his adultery with a wife for whom bridewealth has been paid. People say of such a case that 'the hired labourer does not own the field he tills'. A wife's adultery is sufficient reason for the courts to grant a divorce to the husband in a bridewealth marriage. Pleas for divorce or for the restitution of conjugal rights in such marriages are more often taken to court than are non-bridewealth cases. This is largely owing to ensuing wrangles over bridewealth and rights over children, and also to the more firmly established ties between in-laws which bridewealth helps to create. Other reasons for divorce which a court will usually accept include being struck, even quite lightly, by a wife, desertion by her, her refusal to sleep with her husband or do her household or other customary work, her procuring an abortion and her making any other visits to local medicinal experts without her husband's knowledge and permission. Infertility is not itself sufficient legal cause for divorce in Nyamwezi eyes but, like the death of a child, it often lies behind divorce in practice. A wife can automatically gain a divorce if her husband leaves her for a long time without support or if he seriously injures her, by breaking a limb for example. He is, however, entitled to beat her subject to such limits if she gives him cause. A wife may also

A modern Christian wedding. Such weddings are still not very common.

A group of men playing a game of *isolo* (mankala) during a lull at a wedding.

gain a divorce if her husband is impotent or given to perversion. More generally, it may be added that either spouse who wishes to divorce the other will usually find it possible to do so, either by making the relationship deteriorate until 'just cause' occurs, or simply by insisting firmly on the dissolution of the marriage on grounds of incompatibility.

The incidence of marriage and divorce

Marriage in the Nyamwezi area is an important and a popular though fragile institution. Men usually marry for the first time in their late teens or early twenties, and women usually in their middle to late teens. I have only rarely come across a mature man who never married, and there is almost always some clear physical or psychological handicap involved in such a case. I have no record of a mature woman who has never married and it seems certain that such women are at least extremely rare.

At any point in time, the large majority of adults in the area are married, and some marriages endure for many years and are broken only by death. Divorce is, however, very common in the area. In a sample of 44 men taken in the village of Busangi in Kahama District in 1974–5, 29 (66 per cent) had experienced at least one divorce and the proportion of men with such experience increased, expectably, with age (see Table 4.1).

Table 4.1: Divorce among 44 Busangi men (by age), 1974–5

Age	No.	No. with 1 or more divorces	%
Total range	44	29	66
30 plus	37	28	76
40 plus	31	24	77
50 plus	18	15	83
60 plus	13	12	92

In the case of the men over 60, the only one who had never divorced was a retired Roman Catholic catechist.

It appears from such figures that divorce is in some sense a 'normal' though not necessarily an approved feature of the life-cycle, and further information on the marital histories of these men supports this view. All told they had experienced 139 marriages, of which 50 (some polygynous) were still extant. Eighty (90 per cent) of the 89 previous unions had been broken by divorce. One man had had nine previous wives and another had had eight, while 12 others had had three or four. The 13 men aged 60 and over had experienced 41 divorces (over three per head on average) and the 13 aged from 40–49 had had 21 (average 1.6).

Table 4.2: Types of marriage of 44 Busangi men, 1974–5

	No.	BW	Non-BW	Other
First marriage of husband only	9	1	8	–
First marriage of wife only	24	15	9	–
First marriage of both	35	23	12	–
First marriage of neither	71	14	54	3*
Total	139	53	83	3

*These three were complicated cases. In two bridewealth was paid after many years and in one it is not clear whether it was paid or not.

There is some unevenness in the occurrence of divorce in different sorts of marriage, and some picture of the distribution of forms of marriage themselves is useful at this point (see Table 4.2). It seems clear from these figures that bridewealth is much more often paid for the first marriages of women than for later ones, whereas the difference between the first and later marriages of men is not so marked. The men's figures in fact make most sense when first marriages are looked at in the light of the men's ages (Table 4.3). The table shows a strong shift towards marrying a first wife with bridewealth over the preceding four decades, and this is recognised explicitly by some of the people who argue plausibly enough that it is due to an increase in available wealth during the period in question rather than to any change of preference. It is significant here that many of the men aged over 60 will have married their first wives during the depression years around 1930. It is also interesting that four of these men are among the nine whose first marriages were to previously married women, the remaining five being men of the 40–59 age-group.

The tendency for women's later marriages to be non-bridewealth ones is due to a variety of causes. In some cases it relates quite simply to the woman's age, especially if she is past child-bearing. 'Who would want to pay anything for an old woman like me?' I was once cheerfully asked, in answer to my questions, by one wife in her sixties not long married to a man of similar age. Even if a woman is not very old, however, there is the further factor that her social status is a develop-ing one – despite the fact that she tends in some respects to be a jural minor for her lifetime – and her first marriage is an important threshold in this process of development. A married woman theoreti-cally returns under her father's or her other guardian's authority upon divorce. But people recognise that she is likely to operate more in-dependently than a previously unmarried girl and that this likelihood increases with the length and number of her marriages. Relatedly, it is considered increasingly unreasonable for a man to try to insist upon bridewealth for his daughters' or other wards' later marriages. It may be added that such a woman is known, especially between marriages, by a special term, *mshimbe*, which marks her status as a mature, experienced and comparatively independent woman.

Table 4.3: Types of first marriage of 44 Busangi men (by age), 1974–5

Age at time of survey	BW	Non-BW
20–39	11	2
40–59	10	8
60 plus	3	10
Total	24	20

All this suggests that the degree of control which fathers or other guardians can reasonably hope to exercise over women is an import-ant influence on bridewealth payments. There is much truth in this, but the preferences of husbands are also of some relevance, and these are in fact by no means wholly at odds with those of fathers. The general view of people in the area is that a man's first marriage, at least, should be a bridewealth one – with bridewealth supplied largely by his father – to a previously unmarried girl of good family and good disposition; and it appears from my data that a majority of men's first marriages tend in fact to be to previously unmarried girls for whom bridewealth is paid in most cases. Indeed, I have been told that, even in their later marriages, more men would prefer to marry previously unmarried girls than actually do so. Such girls are, it is said, more malleable and docile than those who have been married before and marriages to them are believed, not wholly fancifully, to be likely to last longer.

The main factors which appear to inhibit more men from achieving marriage to such girls are shortage of the wherewithal for bridewealth and the fact that the time taken to amass it may also render the men less attractive to young women. Nonetheless, it is clear that a considerable number of girls are first married by previously married men. Some of these husbands have simply had a previous history of one or two short marriages. Others are relatively rich men, typically with access to large herds, and they are able to accumulate two or more bridewealth wives polygynously, even though polygyny itself does not depend on bridewealth.

On average it seems that about one man in five in the area has more than one wife at a time. The main features of polygyny there are its instability and the fact that it is by no means simply a prerogative of older men. In one sample group, 24 out of 124 (19 per cent) men were polygynous and the largest section of these were in their forties. The rate dropped fairly severely for men over 50 (from 26 per cent down to 16 per cent), and the second highest group were in fact the 20–29 year olds of whom 21 per cent were polygynous. Far more men have been polygynous than are so at a single point in time. In the sample of 44 men which I referred to earlier, nine (20 per cent) were polygynous at the time of survey but a further 16 (36 per cent) had been so in the past, and whereas only two men out of 13 (15 per cent) over 60 were polygynous, eight others in that group (62 per cent) had previously been so. It appears that polygyny contains its own forces for marital instability additional to those affecting marriages in general. Certainly it is more popular with men than with at least some of their wives, and mutual jealousies and quarrels between co-wives are notorious in the area. All this was vividly brought out for me in an interview in 1975. I was talking to a middle-aged man who had had four wives at one time in the past, and I asked him if he would try to have more than one wife again. Before he could reply, his present wife, who had 'survived' from the conflicts of that polygynous period, sharply butted in and told me 'No, he will not. And I can tell you why. *I* will not put up with it again.' Such outspokenness is rare, for the woman was well known for her unusually strong character; but her sentiments, if not her confidence, appear to be shared by many other women.

Returning at this juncture to the question of divorce, my material suggests that there are subtle differences between the sorts of marriages I have discussed. Thus, although overall men's and women's first marriages appear more or less as likely as their later ones to end in divorce, they do tend to last longer before doing so, and this is especially true of women's first marriages. Bridewealth marriages are also longer lasting and are possibly less prone to dissolution by divorce, but this largely seems to turn on bridewealth's close connection with first marriage. In general, quite the most stable unions are women's first marriages with bridewealth, whereas bridewealth marriages to previously married women and women's first marriages without bridewealth are not significantly longer lasting or less prone to divorce than others. Table 4.4 based on the 136 marriages in Table 4.2 for which adequate information was available sets out some of these trends.

Table 4.4: Stability of women's marriages*

	Total	Divorces	Still extant after 5 years or more
Women's first marriages with BW	38	13	18
Women's first marriages without BW	21	16	3
Women's later marriages with BW	15	9	3
Women's later marriages without BW	62	40	9

* Marriages ended by death or extant after less than five years are not shown.

The functions and significance of marriage

We have seen that there is quite a range of ways and circumstances in which people come to marry, and I have tried so far to bring out the main normative and distributional aspects of this situation. I turn now to a review of some more general features of the institution which have to varying degrees emerged from the material I have presented.

It is clear that marriage in the area is deeply concerned with reproduction and child-rearing, and with the creation of ties of affinity and kinship. It is also clear that it has much to do with the establishment of ordered sexual relations in society, and that it is closely involved in

Nyamwezi processes of making a living. None of these concerns of marriage is, of course, particularly surprising in itself, but it is perhaps worthwhile to look at the relationship between them and attempt to assess their relative importance, since this has been the subject of considerable debate in comparative discussions of marriage in general.[4] Some writers have stressed relatively stable sexual relations as the crucial element in marriage, while others have more strongly emphasised affinity or reproduction. Others again have argued that marriage is essentially a bundle of functions and rights which may vary in detail from one society to another. There is in fact something to be said for all these viewpoints, which are not all quite as incompatible as might at first appear. In the Nyamwezi case, it can be argued that the sexual and reproductive sides of marriage are each in their own way the crucial thing about the institution, and that from another angle marriage essentially *combines* a range of functions.

One general point of some importance in this context is that marriage has a time dimension. Any marriage – Nyamwezi or other – which lasts any length of time is bound to change, and some ingredient activities increase while others wane. Moreover, with a high divorce rate of the sort I have described, marriages may start at many different points in the life-cycle. Two factors help reduce the complications of this time dimension to order. One is the idea of sequence and the other lies in the relation between 'real' and 'ideal'. A contemporarily sexless marriage which has had a sexual component in its earlier days is clearly different from one in which a sexual relationship was absent from the start. Again, a marriage late in life is not likely to be subject to the same expectations, with regards to childbirth for example, as a union between young people, so that a greater degree of leeway between ideal and reality will sensibly be tolerated in such cases.

A further aspect of the situation is uncovered by this last point. For the decision about whether or not 'a marriage is a marriage' is to a great extent one for the parties to the union themselves. Proof of a woman's adultery is sufficient grounds for her Nyamwezi husband to divorce her and in this sense her marriage no longer exists after this. Yet her husband may decide to overlook the matter and the marriage then continues. Or a woman whose husband fails to keep up sexual relations with her may decide that this is or is not sufficient reason to embark on a divorce.

I have said that sex and reproduction each have a good claim to be the crucial elements in Nyamwezi marriage. With regard to sex, a marriage which has not been sexually consummated is in most local eyes no marriage at all, though it may take time for it to collapse. No matter how much ceremonial has been performed or how much bride-wealth has been paid, the general view is that a marriage does not technically exist without sexual intercourse. Consistently with this, a man who takes a wife through others' pressures, for example a reluctant heir of a dead brother's wife, may aptly show his own mind on the issue by refusing to have intercourse with her and this is likely, even if she is quite old, to lead to her withdrawal from the union. People often talk of such a woman, and of others who are sexually neglected by their husbands, as a wife 'in name only'.

The situation with regard to reproduction is rather different. The failure of a marriage to be fruitful may be quite distressing and may lead to its collapse, but it is, as I have mentioned earlier, a much less legitimate reason for divorce than sexual failure. It can be argued, moreover, that marriage is not even the only way in which legitimate links between a man and his children and their maternal kin can be established, since the child of an unmarried mother can be redeemed if its father can establish his paternity.

On the other hand, while agreeing that a marriage must be sexually consummated and need not, legally, be fruitful, knowledgeable local commentators nonetheless assert that reproduction is the most important single element in marriage. This paradox largely turns on different emphases in the idea of the 'crucial' or 'important'. With sex, we are dealing with a necessary condition of marriage – and indeed of reproduction, though its significance cannot be reduced simply to this. As such it is a vital but not necessarily the most highly valued element in the institution. In reproduction, we have something which is recognised as not wholly essential but which is still very highly esteemed.

The question of what lies behind the esteem is a complex one. In conversations on this issue, the point was made to me that more was involved here than the most direct result of childbirth whereby a man and his wife jointly became parents. Highly significant though this was, there was the further fact that a considerably wider range of persons were lastingly involved with each other through their mutual relationship to the child. The birth of children was thus also seen as creating kinship and as reinforcing the ties between those previously only linked by marriage. Indeed, it appears that when affinal ties are strengthened in this way, they may well persist even beyond the divorce of the married couple themselves, so that, for instance, a father may still be warmly greeted and referred to as 'our son-in-law' by his wife's kin long after his divorce from her. In contrast, when a childless marriage concludes in a divorce, that is most likely to end the affair for all concerned.

One should perhaps be careful in this context not to place excessive weight upon affinity since, with the main exception of chiefs and other prominent 'royals', there is little to suggest that political or economic alliance regularly plays a large part in the choice of marriage partners. Relations between in-laws are useful ones – the term *nkwilima* for a son-in-law appears to mean literally 'the in-law who cultivates' (for his wife's father) – and their existence should be given recognition along with the husband–wife tie itself on which I have mainly focussed my account. This latter focus is itself, however, not simply an ethnocentric one, on my part, since a great deal of what is understood by and entailed in marriage in the area most directly concerns the two spouses. Again, we have already seen some evidence that marriage and affinity are not simply one and the same thing there. The very persistence of affinity beyond divorce, or one may add beyond a spouse's death, in part attests to this, as does the possibility of establishing legitimate relations between a man and his children's maternal kin through redemption payments without any marriage. It may also be recalled here that whereas the verb 'to marry' (*kutola*) is used only with respect to taking a wife (in either bridewealth or non-bridewealth marriage), the word *kukwa* is used both for marrying with bridewealth (but not without) and for making redemption payments for children born either in non-bridewealth marriage or out of wedlock altogether. The distinction between these two terms and their usage seems to fit well with that between marriage and affinity in the area and with the fact that affinity is at its strongest when it has been buttressed by the birth of children.[5]

Such then are the rival claims of sex and reproduction as the cornerstone of Nyamwezi marriage. It is, I hope, not difficult to see that these claims are not wholly incompatible and, indeed, that they can jointly co-exist with the idea of marriage as a composite of many parts. The truth of this is visible in the wide range of reasons which are held to be sufficient for divorce; and it runs well with the diffuse and multifunctional nature of familial ties in this and other societies. In addition, the same point emerges from the deep involvement of marriage, and the households built upon it, in the processes of gaining a living from the land and in the domestic economy in general. For although marriage is not typically defined locally in terms of this involvement, it is clear that quantitatively a large part of Nyamwezi married life is normally devoted to it by both spouses. Indeed, it is possible to argue in this context that the marriage system, and the social and economic control over women which goes with it, are the crucial domestic-level supports for the ecologically important freedom of movement which men have till recently enjoyed in this area; for they provide a man with the possibility of establishing, and through polygyny perhaps expanding, his own viable domestic enterprise in a village community without the necessity of daily contact with and aid from local kinsfolk (cf. Chapter 3 and Abrahams, 1978). I suspect, moreover, that even divorce, which places limits on such possibilities, may well also be related paradoxically to the same phenomena. For the fragility of marriage seems to be consistent with the seasonal intensity of the production process and with the usufructory nature of land holding which precludes the possibility for a married couple of their being bound together by their joint interest in the possession and development of a heritable estate in land. The local saying that 'a man who drives away his wife in the rainy season is a fool' perhaps adds weight to this conjecture, if only by its implication that there really is a better time and place for such an act, and the fact that chiefs used often to restrict the hearing of divorce cases to the relative quiet of the dry season because of their particularly disruptive effect on agriculture in the rains is also of some interest here (cf. Abrahams, 1967a, p. 102).

Household and homestead

Before the re-organisations of 1974–5 homesteads occasionally contained a dozen or more people, though they were usually somewhat smaller than this. As we have seen, they typically consisted of a man and his wife or wives, their resident children and sometimes a spouse and children of one or more of these. One or two other relatives such as the mother, or a sister or younger brother, or a sister's child of the homestead head might also be present. Although the male and female members, with the exception of small children, usually ate separately, homesteads were the largest units in which members of one sex ate together regularly throughout the year.

Such homesteads contained one or more households, and a household was a distinct food-producing, food-owning, and child-rearing

109

unit, though households of the same homestead often co-operated in such matters. The household was the basic economic unit and, as I have mentioned, the husband–wife relationship was its key structural element. Ideally, every wife had her own hut and household.

Since 1974–5 (and earlier in some *ujamaa* villages) these customary arrangements have been somewhat modified, as I have briefly noted in the previous chapter. One main tendency has been for household and homestead group to coincide more closely. Thus, in the new village of Busangi, which began in 1974, each one-acre plot typically contained a homestead occupied by a single household, though people who had previously occupied joint homesteads often had adjacent plots. It may be noted that this tends to produce a pattern, comparable to that in many parts of Europe, in which nuclear families tend to be the basic co-resident groups. It is not yet clear how radical a change this is, and much seems likely to depend on the extent of the future development of permanent dwellings and other forms of household wealth which may serve to divide individual families yet more sharply from each other. It is, however, possibly of some interest here that the term *familia* has become a regular term for such household groups in local planning jargon, and it is beginning to be heard occasionally in the conversations of villagers themselves. The projected development of co-operative enterprise in the new villages is, of course, a further and in part possibly a countervailing factor of some relevance in this context as my discussion of *ujamaa* villages suggests. I will return to this point later. As we have seen, however, such communal patterns do not yet constitute a substantial part of agricultural co-operation in the area, and for the present the basic co-operating units in the great majority of villages remain relatively autonomous households with male heads.

The activities of households in general and of husbands and wives in particular tend to follow the customary sexual division of labour. Most heavy work is done by men when need for it arises, while a majority of everyday tasks are performed by women. Thus men do bush-clearing and the preparation of new plots, threshing, cutting firewood, and most building work. Women do most secondary plot preparation, planting, weeding and most of the preparation of food. As late as 1960 women usually ground their own flour by hand, but the situation had changed radically by 1974. By that time mechanical mills were available in most areas and most women had firmly refused to continue with hand-grinding and now had their flour ground at these.[6] It was normal for them to carry the grain to the mill themselves, but some managed to get men to help them do this on occasions when a mill broke down and a more distant one had to be used temporarily. All this is consistent with the fact that the division of labour is a source of power for women which provides, through men's dependence upon them within it, some possibility for them to negotiate and mitigate the demands made of them in a still largely male-dominated social system.

Kinship

Kinship (*budugu*) among the Nyamwezi is not a difficult concept for a European observer. It concerns essentially relations between persons who are or who consider themselves to be linked genealogically by a parent–child relationship or through a series of them, and such relationships should ideally possess both a jural and a physical base. The ties so formed are expected to be characterised by various behavioural patterns, some common to all and others more specific, such as the use of kinship terms, the provision of help when it is needed, and respect between parents and children. As elsewhere some kin, in the genealogical sense, do not behave in the right way, and the patterns of behaviour expected between kin are also sometimes extended to others. Such extensions and shortcomings do not, I think, affect the validity of positing a genealogical base to Nyamwezi kinship, though they are of course still important at the practical level.

If Nyamwezi kinship in itself is not especially puzzling, the Nyamwezi kinship *system* has proved rather more so, for it is not easily described by the labels – e.g. patrilineal, matrilineal, cognatic – which are commonly in use in social anthropological accounts.[7] By 'kinship system' here I mean the structural ordering of kin ties *vis-à-vis* each other and *vis-à-vis* those of marriage, and the best approach to this in the Nyamwezi case is to view the system as a *combination* of a range of structural and behavioural features. These mainly take the form of oppositions between male and female, proximal and alternate generations, joking and avoidance, familiarity and respect, and kinship and marriage themselves.

The distinction between male and female is an obvious one which all kinship systems and, indeed, all social systems recognise, but the way in which they do so varies very much from one case to the next. In the Nyamwezi case the distinction is quite highly marked, though it is

111

not used systematically to determine recruitment to bounded groups whose membership is based upon descent traced from a common ancestor. For, with the partial exception of the 'royal families' which flourished as powerful minorities in a changing range of forms until the end of the colonial period, such descent groups have not been a regular feature of the social structure of the area.

A fundamental feature of the distinction in the Nyamwezi case is the fact already touched upon that rights in the productive and reproductive capacity of females are customarily largely held by males and are transferable between them through bridewealth and related payments. No comparable payments are made between women for rights over males or indeed other females, and it is of course consistent with this that one finds polygyny, but not polyandry, in the area and that sexual relations outside marriage are a recognised offence for wives, but not for husbands unless they infringe the rights of other men. Looked at in these terms, the position of women in this system approximates much more closely than that of men to the status of perpetual jural minors. We have seen that the degree of self-determination which can be enjoyed by women does in fact increase with age and marital experience; and having adult sons can be a help. The division of labour is a source of some strength to them, and I have already mentioned a few possible tendencies for change which are at work in the new villages. The overall picture still remains much the same, however, and it is supported by the further fact that most property, including its most valuable forms, is held and inherited by men. In addition, although diviners are occasionally women, access to divination for a woman is largely controlled by her male kinsfolk and her husband.

A second major feature of the distinction between males and females in this case is that relations traced through them differ from and complement each other in important ways. This too turns on bridewealth and related payments. Ideally, it can be argued, the system is one in which control over children is mainly vested in their mother's husband – who should be their genitor – and his kin. This is the case in most bridewealth marriages, though complications may arise through adultery and divorce, but the situation is of course quite different in non-bridewealth unions in which children belong to their mother's kin unless they are redeemed. The sons of bridewealth marriages, or others who have been redeemed, may expect to inherit property from their father and perhaps from other patrikin. Unredeemed sons have to look to their mother's people for inheritance, though there are sometimes problems here since the sons of such kin may exert a prior claim if they themselves are born of bridewealth unions or have been redeemed. It is clear that individual cases may differ widely from each other in these ways. Overall, however, it is true to say that any particular person's ties to or through his or her father will differ significantly at any point in time from those to his or her mother's people.

In addition to sex, a person's generational position is an important determinant of relationships with others in this kinship system. The general rule is one of opposition between proximal generations and alliance and identification between alternate ones. This runs closely with a behavioural distinction which the people make between two categories of persons called *basoni* and *bapugu*. The term *basoni*, which derives from a word *nsoni* meaning 'shame', refers to those with whom one should behave respectfully and formally; and in the case of some relationships through marriage actual avoidance may be practised. In contrast, the term *bapugu* refers to those with whom one should behave familiarly and, in some cases, engage in regular joking and teasing.

In general, kin in proximal generations treat each other in a sober and respectful manner, and poking fun and making reference to sex are normally avoided between them. This fits well with the authority and control which the parental generation exercise, and this in turn makes for an important element of asymmetry in the relationships concerned, especially if the people involved are fairly closely related to each other. In the cases of mother-in-law and son-in-law, and father-in-law and daughter-in-law, avoidance of any direct interaction may be practised at least in the early years of marriage, and a father-in-law may even refuse to utter his daughter-in-law's name. I have seen a man get up and stand with his face close to the wall when a woman married to a relative of the junior proximal generation came into the room, and it is usual for sons-in-law to take great care to avoid any direct confrontation between themselves and their wife's mother and other close female relatives of the mother's generation. Such 'avoidance behaviour' is of course widespread in other areas and it should be viewed as an expression of extreme respect which is intended to preclude rather than reflect or engender hostility.

Familiarity and joking mark relationships between the members of alternate generations. Grandparents and grandchildren take delight in making mild fun of each other, and those of opposite sex may refer to each other jokingly as husband and wife, especially when the grandchildren are young. Girls often share their secrets with a grandmother, and conversation is generally much freer between members of the two generations than between parents and children and their peers. This freedom and familiarity is usually extended to the spouses of grandchildren as long as the marital relationship is sound, but it may be switched off if serious conflict between husband and wife develops.

To some extent the members of alternate generations see themselves as one, and this of course makes sense in terms of their shared relation to the generation in between. It is common for children to be given a grandparent's name and babies are often said to cry until they get one. Grandparents often talk of themselves as being reborn in their grandchildren, and although the idea is more a figurative one than a literal belief in reincarnation, it does seem to contribute to the perceived continuity and content of an individual's identity.

Joking is also characteristic of relations between in-laws of the same generation, and between brothers-in-law one may even find some horseplay. In the case of kin, however, intra-generational relationships – and especially those between siblings – tend to be influenced by the further factor of relative seniority and authority, and this tends to give them a more formal and more serious tone. The authority element in the brother–sister tie becomes particularly important once their father or other guardian in the parental generation has died, since the brother will then assume quasi-parental responsibilities, e.g. with regard to bridewealth payments and repayments for his sister's marriages. At such a juncture even relations between brothers-in-law may start to take on the formality which usually marks the link between a father and his daughter's husband.

For completeness' sake, two cases may be mentioned here where joking actually takes place between persons who are technically in the next generation to each other. The first is between a young man and his mother's brother's wife and it is said to derive from the fact that he may well inherit her if her husband dies. In practice, however, such inheritance is rather rare and the customary joking is not easy to explain, apart from the pleasure which it gives to the participants. Such joking is known to occur elsewhere, typically in the company of joking with the mother's brother himself.[8] In the Nyamwezi case, however, the mother's brother is treated with the respect due to the parental generation generally, and this of course makes sense in terms

114

of his real or potential authority over his sister's children. The second sort of case involves a man and the son of a distant male kinsman of the same generation. The son will typically be classed as 'child' within the Nyamwezi terminology and his mother will be called a 'sister-in-law'. In such cases the familiarity which characterises such brother-in-law/sister-in-law relationships may be vicariously extended to the son, who may for instance even as a teenager be asked jokingly on his arrival whether he has just been suckling at his mother's breast. The purpose of such joking seems to be to stress the relative absence of authority between the two distantly related kinsmen and thus override the generational difference.

Kinship in general, notwithstanding the internal distinctions which I have been making, is marked by an ideal at least of moral commitment and mutual aid which should be given as and when required without emphasis upon the need to give exact return. As I have already noted, it is in these terms that the people contrast kinship ties with those of neighbourhood. On the other hand, we have seen that kin by no means necessarily live near each other, and this to some extent reflects the potential for conflict between them over property and other matters. Such conflict may receive expression in the form of witchcraft accusations, though I have noted that the incidence of these is not at all confined to the kinship sphere and neighbours also may be feared as witches. Unless they are quite closely related, links between kin who live far apart tend to lapse and be forgotten in the course of time. Genealogically close kin are expected to keep in touch even over a considerable distance, and they should visit each other from time to time as well as keeping each other informed of births, marriages, sicknesses and deaths, and other matters of mutual concern. In one court case I witnessed, a man who contested the inheritance of a dead kinsman's property was told that he had allowed kinship 'to die' by failing to keep regular contact with the deceased, and this contributed to his losing the case. It should be noted, however, that the 'death' of kinship in this sense is merely relative, and his entitlement would not have been forfeited had it not been in competition with that of another close kinsman who had maintained an active link with the dead man.

The waning of particular kinship ties is of some practical relevance for the final opposition that I wish to deal with here, *viz.* that between kinship and marriage. This finds its most clear expression in the rule already mentioned that known kin should not marry. This rule is plausibly associated by some of the people with the idea that bridewealth and redemption payments should not be made in any particular case by anyone who might conceivably receive them, and this of course emphasises the property element in kinship relations and the fact that even distant kinsmen are potentially each other's heirs, if nearer relatives are lacking. Although the rule applies in theory to all kin, its efficient application is affected by a variety of factors, and it is occasionally bent or broken especially if there is neither a close genealogical nor active tie between the parties. With the exception noted earlier of some Sumbwa, a close genealogical link when known is an effective barrier even if the relationship has not been activated for some time, but there can be argument when an operational relationship is not strongly supported genealogically. The outcome then depends upon the attitudes of the main parties involved and the pressures which may be brought to bear upon them by others. In some cases, the potential direct recipients of bridewealth may, understandably, be rather more in favour of a marriage than those who will have to pay the bulk of it. The prohibition on marriage between kin also applies to sexual relations generally. This rule is, however, broken rather more often than the marriage rule, both because of the more public nature of marriage and because many young people who engage in sexual adventures are less well informed than their elders about who their kinsfolk are.

The opposition between kinship and marriage and the other structural features which I have discussed are reflected in some aspects of the kinship terminology which is outlined in Figure 3 (a–d). The terminology is basically of the kind known as Iroquoian (since the type was first documented among the Iroquois Indians of North America), and among its chief characteristics are separate terminologies for kin and in-laws, and a merging of some terms for the members of alternate generations. Different terms are used for proximal and alternate generations and in the proximal generation links through males are generally clearly distinguished from those traced through females. Within an individual's own generation, same-sex siblings and some cousins are clearly distinguished from those of opposite sex and they are also distinguished from each other by virtue of their seniority or juniority to 'ego'.

Forces and directions of change

Although the situation which I have described is still mainly the

Figure 3a. Nyamwezi kinship terminology (reference terms, *male* ego)

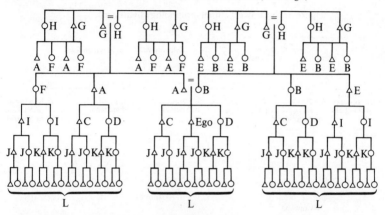

A. Dada (Uso = your father, Ise = his or her father)
B. Mayu (Noko = your mother, Nina = his or her mother)
C. Nkulu if senior, Nzuna if junior to ego
D. Ilumbu
E. Mami
F. Sengi
G. Guku

H. Mama
I. Myala (sibling terms are
   sometimes used)
J. Mwana
K. Mwipwa
L. Mwizukulu

Figure 3b. Nyamwezi kinship terminology (reference terms, *female* ego)

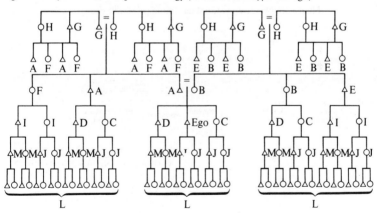

A. Dada (Uso = your father, Ise = his or her father)
B. Mayu (Noko = your mother, Nina = his or her mother)
C. Nkulu if senior, Nzuna if junior to ego
D. Ilumbu
E. Mami
F. Sengi
G. Guku

H. Mama
I. Myala (sibling terms are
   sometimes used)
J. Mwana
L. Mwizukulu
M. Nsengizana

117

Figure 3c. Nyamwezi affinal terminology (*male* ego)

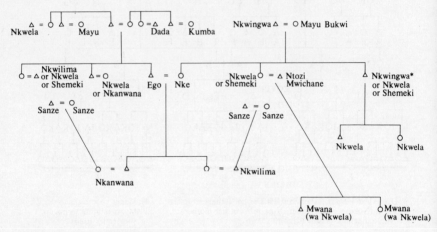

*Wife's brother may be called *Nkwingwa* if he is senior to wife, and especially if wife's father is dead. *Shemeki* is a Swahili term.

Figure 3d. Nyamwezi affinal terminology (*female* ego)

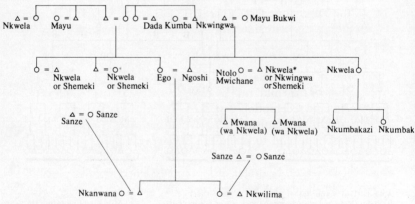

*Husband's brother may be called Nkwingwa if he is senior to husband, and especially if husband's father is dead.

118

current one, it will be clear from my account that a variety of forces for change are in operation in the area. This is of course no new thing for the Nyamwezi, and the people will no doubt continue to adapt themselves and their society to the pressures and the opportunities which come their way. As I have from time to time brought out, the developing legal and court system and the changes at the village level are probably the most important factors now at work in the present context of kinship and marriage. It would be foolhardy to try to predict the outcome of their influence with any certainty, if only because both emanate from central government and either of them might conceivably be subject to reform; but it would be at least equally foolhardy to ignore them, and it seems worthwhile to try to perceive the broad directions in which they are pushing.

One main direction here is towards a greater degree of equality of status between men and women. To some extent this is a conscious policy – there is a women's wing of CCM (and previously of TANU) operative in the towns and in some rural areas, and special Women's Development Officers are also to be found there, though they do not seem to be very effective as yet at the village level. In 1975, President Nyerere even suggested publicly that it might be time to give up polygyny – for social and moral rather than religious reasons. Polygyny, however, albeit subject to a husband's declaration of intent, is still enshrined in the relatively recent national marriage law which is expected to be applied throughout the country in due course, and for the present one should perhaps look to other sections of this law for more immediate signs of change. Its most important points in this regard are the relative equality of status which it ascribes to each spouse with respect to rights to children and their custody, and the determination of these rights by reference to the spouse's behaviour and the 'interests of the child' rather than to automatic consequences of bridewealth and redemption payments. This law is as yet only partly and haphazardly administered, when at all, in rural courts which, I have mentioned, tend to make use of a growingly unpredictable mixture of local and wider custom. Its effects upon Nyamwezi marriage will, however, be drastic if it becomes generally administered and one result of this may well be an increased reluctance to bring marriage cases to the formal courts. The collusion of both parties to a dispute would, however, be essential for such reluctance to be effective, and there would be many cases in which this was unobtainable. I am told that awareness of some aspects of this law is leading to a fall-off in redemption payments, but it is hard to check this. Certainly, there appears to be no decrease in the incidence of bridewealth marriage, and other factors, such as prestige, the availability of wealth, and the control which the parental generation can exercise over younger girls, are still clearly important.

I have already mentioned that the development of collective agricultural projects in some villages is permitting women to participate in the rural economy as individuals rather than as wives. Such women are entitled to individual share of the proceeds of such projects based upon the days and hours which they have devoted to them and, at least ideally, what they do with this is their affair. Once again, any major increase in such practices will be likely to affect the power structure within marriage in the area very seriously, and people are aware of this though there was not much anxiety about it in 1975 since such projects were so few. More generally, it is perhaps worth adding here that many Nyamwezi men are aware of the ways in which their social and economic organisation favours them against women, though they are equally aware of the power which a woman can derive from sources like the division of labour and, allegedly, from witchcraft to which women are said to be specially partial. This last view appears likely to reflect some elements of male feelings of guilt on this issue. One thoughtful friend of mine once admitted in a conversation that the system is by no means wholly fair to women, but he added ruefully: 'What can we do? If we gave them their freedom, they'd destroy us in revenge.'

Another possible result of changes at the village level is a narrowing of the range of effective co-operation between relatives. One aspect of this is the tendency I noted earlier for household and homestead to coincide, though this does not in itself necessarily involve serious problems of inter-household co-operation, and, indeed, experience from this and other areas of the world suggests that actual co-residence of kin can all too easily engender conflicts which reduce effective close co-operation.[9] There is, however, the further possibility that co-operation between relatives who live in different villages will be reduced, the more people find themselves practically and even contractually bound to devote themselves to operations in their own village. As I have described, this possibility was again most noticeable in 1974–5 in *ujamaa* villages with collective projects, since it was technically necessary for people in such communities to obtain permission to take time off for visits to non-village relatives. This was not radically different from the pre-*ujamaa* need to give priority to one's immediate short-term responsibilities to neighbours in jobs like millet-threshing, as against one's more general and diffuse obligations to kin. The crucial question is, however, one of scale, and any significant increase in the scope of corporate activities within villages seems bound to place some strain both on kinship reciprocity, despite its ideals of long-term commitment, and on interaction between in-laws also. Truly collective village enterprises are, as I have noted, few, but it seems clear that if the new forms of village organisation and management are to work they will in any case demand more time and energy from villagers than have previous forms; and of course the very pattern of spatial nucleation is in part designed to inspire a concomitant pattern of 'nucleated' interests and activities. It remains only to add that although such a development might help to bring village 'family' units closer together at the same time as it divides them from their kin and affines elsewhere, experience indicates that there is also a considerable potential for conflict in such closeness.

5   The Nyamwezi in the wider world

Participation in the nation

Although the previous chapters have, naturally enough, concentrated on the description and analysis of structures, processes and events among the Nyamwezi and their neighbours in the Nyamwezi area itself, it will be quite clear from my account of these that an involvement with the wider world has been a major feature of the people's life for well over a hundred years. By the middle of the nineteenth century, trading connections to the coast and also inland to such areas as Karagwe and Katanga, to the north-west and south-west respectively, were already well established; and through these the Nyamwezi were by that time well acquainted with a wide variety of other areas and peoples, as a result both of their own travels and of their reception of outsiders – mainly African and Arab but also Indian and, later, European – into Unyamwezi itself.

Such early contacts and their subsequent development clearly had far-reaching effects upon the people and their country. Politically, these ranged from the acquisition in the early days of conus-shells which then became the main regalia of chiefship,[1] to the gradual secularisation of chiefly office and its eventual inclusion, as I have described, within the framework of British and German colonial rule. Economically, the people were drawn into an ever-widening network of exchange relationships which, in differing forms, have since then always complemented and at times competed with their efforts to produce food for subsistence. Within the field of social structure, the open quality of Nyamwezi society, which I have stressed at many points in my account, has been both a positive reaction to such contacts with the outside world and an important condition of their successful growth; and culturally also, the people have imported a great deal, including some forms of dance and divination and an extensive array of spirit-possession and other societies and cults.

When one's focus is primarily upon the people and their country, and when outside influence includes two major European powers and two major wars between them, it is all too easy to assume that the only

122

processes deserving serious attention are those in which the wider world has penetrated into and has made its mark on Unyamwezi. It should already have begun to be apparent, however, that the Nyamwezi have been by no means simply the passive recipients of external influence, and it is perhaps worthwhile to say more about this. In the first place, when they have not wished for it, they have quite often sought ways to resist such influence. Sometimes their resistance took a violent form as when Isike, chief of Unyanyembe, fought the Germans, albeit unsuccessfully, early in the 1890s;[2] and sometimes it has been more subtle as when TANU cards and propaganda were smuggled in the 1950s from Kahama into Geita District where the party had officially been banned from pursuing its activities.[3] Secondly, when they have been more positively disposed towards such influence, the people have quite actively encouraged it and helped create a favourable environment for its development among them. The people's harnessing of indigenous forms of neighbourhood co-operation to help establish TANU at the village level in 1958–9 is a good example of this which I witnessed at first hand and have described elsewhere (Abrahams, 1967a, Ch. 8), and one may also mention again here their much earlier role in the development of trading contacts with the outside world.

There is rather more, however, to the situation than such matters of resistance to, or constructive participation in, the importation of new ideas, goods and social forms and forces into Unyamwezi. There is also the important question of the people's own substantial contribution to new and wider forms of social group and institution and, more generally, the considerable part which they have played in helping to change the life of others. For instance, in the ivory and slave trading and in the fighting which marked the violent middle decades of the nineteenth century in East and Central Africa their role clearly had, with that of others, quite far-reaching repercussions. These extended all the way down to the coast from the interior villages of those with whom they fought and traded, and they ultimately reached the homes of those in Europe and America who took pleasure in the music of ivory-keyed pianos, the grace of new cutlery handles, or a game of billiards in elegant surroundings. Less tangibly, perhaps, though equally significantly, their travels at that time were also helping to create the web of friendships, business links and even formal 'joking partnerships' (*utani*) between themselves and other groups which in turn helped to foster – along with subsequent

123

participation in and resistance to colonialism – the awareness of bonds well beyond those of the village or the chiefdom on which the social unity of modern Tanzania now depends.

Friendship, even in the form of blood-brotherhood which it often took in this area, and business links which were sometimes cemented by marriage,[4] are fairly commonplace phenomena and, although they are of course no less significant for that, I will not say more about them here. The joking partnerships which I have mentioned are, however, much less widespread institutions; and the extent of their development among the Nyamwezi and some other Tanzanian peoples has rarely been matched elsewhere, although joking is a very common feature of the ties between some relatives in many kinship systems including of course that of the Nyamwezi themselves. Joking partnerships are recognised between the Nyamwezi and a number of other Tanzanian peoples, including the Zaramu and Zigua who, significantly, lie between the Nyamwezi and the coast. The relationships typically involve privileged verbal abuse, and in the past at least considerable horseplay, between those participating in them, and it is important that such joking partners should not take offence at what is said or done to them. In the past there was also typically an exchange of services, accompanied by such abuse, on ritual occasions such as funerals. According to most accounts the partnerships arose originally out of an earlier state of hostility between members of the participating groups, and it seems possible that they were modelled upon similar forms of relationship between chiefdoms, dynasties and clans within the groups concerned. Their function, like that of ceremonial exchange in other areas of the world such as New Guinea, appears to have been the establishment of peaceful and fruitful interaction between groups of people whose relationships to each other could otherwise easily be marked by unpredictability, tension and violence.[5] Clearly, the creation of wider state structures has modified the need for such mechanisms for keeping peace and promoting co-operation, but the relationships still retain some of their force even today. One reason for this is that *utani* joking is often a source of considerable amusement and pleasure to participants and audience alike; but the links also still provide a useful basis on which members of the groups concerned can seek and receive help when visiting a distant place or coming as relative strangers into an urban or any other social setting with a diverse population, such as a rural sisal estate. Thus when one of my Nyamwezi friends came down to Dar es

Salaam to visit me just before I left in 1975, he asked a Zaramu man the way to the University. When the man heard he was a Nyamwezi he started joking with him and accompanied him a long way on the route there out of town to make sure he would reach his destination without further difficulty.

The establishment of the colonial state, like that of independent Tanzania which followed it, provided a variety of new opportunities for Nyamwezi and other Tanzanians to participate in a wider world. Some, such as recruitment into armed and ancillary services during the First and Second World Wars, were no doubt less welcome than others, though the experience of travel, for example to Kenya and in some cases as far afield as Burma, was a valuable and valued one for some men I have known. During peace-time many villagers, as we have seen, also went to work at different periods as labour migrants on sisal estates in Tanga and surrounding Districts, on clove estates in Pemba, and later to the cotton-growing areas of Sukumaland.

These patterns of participation in the wider economy and polity were by their nature open to large numbers of Nyamwezi, or at least to large numbers of Nyamwezi men. Their long experience and with it their good reputation as travellers and workers no doubt helped them to compete well with others as a source of potentially reliable labour in the migrant labour market. Moreover, the work itself usually needed a large labour force and was often hard and not especially attractive except as a source of cash which was not readily available elsewhere in more congenial surroundings.

The colonial period also saw the beginning of higher level Nyamwezi participation in the actual 'management' of the developing state and its institutions. School teachers and clerks were already being trained under the Germans, and after the disturbance of the First World War, which was partly fought on Nyamwezi soil, educational and other services began again under the British and the training of an African administrative cadre started afresh. One of the most significant features of this process in the Nyamwezi area was the relatively large share of educational facilities which the chiefly families gained from an early date. To some extent, of course, this was due to a clear perception by at least some chiefs of the value of formal education for their children; but their privileged position no doubt made it easier for them both to see this and to realise their wishes than it was for many ordinary people, and they also in fact received much help and encouragement from Government. The founding of the

Government School in Tabora in 1925 was an important event in this context for, as I have briefly noted, the school was originally established mainly for the sons of Nyamwezi and other chiefs who seemed likely to succeed to their father's office in due course.[6] The school, which was sometimes called the Eton of Tanganyika in its early days, was opened to all comers in 1933, but the idea that good education was important for the sons of chiefs was by that time well established and many of them still continued to be sent there or to other secondary schools such as the Roman Catholic St Mary's, which was also in Tabora.

Although some of these sons of chiefs distinguished themselves in other spheres – Yunge Mwanansali, for example, was the captain of Tanganyika's first international football team and was one of the first Tanganyikans to rise to a high position in East African Railways – several of them entered political and administrative life, and most of these also became chiefs at some point in their career. The participation of such men in the political life of the nation reached its high point in the years before and just around the time of Independence. Abdallah Fundikira, who succeeded to the large Unyanyembe chiefdom in Tabora District in 1957 after higher education at Makerere and a period of service as an Agricultural Officer, became a member of the Legislative Council in 1958 and held a variety of Ministerial appointments from 1959 to 1962, before becoming Chairman of East African Airways for a time and then retiring into private life. Nsabila Lugusha of Ngulu in Tabora District also went on from school to Makerere and became chief in 1942. In the late 1950s he was made a member of the Legislative Council and held posts as Assistant Minister for Local Government and Deputy Speaker of the Council in the period just prior to Independence, shortly after which he fell into disgrace. Another chief, Kasanda of Unyambiyu in the present-day Igunga District, worked in Provincial Administration until he became chief in 1943. He subsequently served on national committees concerned with game reserves and education and he also visited Uganda as an official representative of Tanganyika when the Owens Fall hydroelectric scheme was opened in 1954. A fourth chief, Humbi Ziota of Busongo in Igunga District, has a very long record of distinguished service which stretches to the present day. After working as a clerk in East African Railways and Harbours and in the Provincial Administration, he became chief in 1944 and he has held a wide variety of posts during his career. He was

Assistant Minister for Natural Resources in 1957–9, and he has since then served at different times as Regional Commissioner in Morogoro and Shinyanga, as Chairman of the Tanzania Tobacco Authority, and as an elected Member of Parliament representing the constituency of his home District. Like Lugusha and Kasanda (and indeed Yunge), Humbi was a student at Tabora School, and all those I have mentioned also visited Britain either on courses or in an official capacity during the 1950s. The high level of such participation in national political affairs can to some extent be gauged from the fact that in 1957 two of these men, Humbi and Lugusha, were among the first three Africans in Tanganyika to be appointed to any ministerial posts, and in 1958 a third, Fundikira, was the African candidate elected to represent the whole of the then Western Province, which included Unyamwezi, as a TANU-supported member of the Legislative Council.

Humbi Ziota is still an MP and a nationally respected figure, as too is the rather younger Louis Sazia, son of Andrea Mhanda the former chief of Ngogwa in Kahama District. Sazia, who did not become chief himself, is MP for Kahama East and he has also served both as a Regional Commissioner and as the Chairman of the National Housing Bank. Nonetheless, it appears that the extent of Nyamwezi recruitment into positions of political leadership at the national level has declined somewhat since the early 1960s, and as far as I can tell no Nyamwezi has been appointed to a Ministerial post in the Government since 1963. The reasons for this shift are not wholly clear and it is of course quite hard to generalise about fluctuations in small numbers of this sort which can easily be affected by particular individuals' decisions and contingent events. It is, however, tempting to suggest that the relative lack historically of other power bases besides chiefship in the area has been of some importance in this context. After Independence, as I have described, TANU, which had earlier resisted the establishment of a 'second house' of chiefs at national level, set about replacing chiefship with new forms of administrative office at the local level; and this move away from both hereditary and local power bases was no doubt difficult for some chiefs to adapt to, and may even have affected their efficacy and loyalty at higher levels in one or two cases. Yet, if the policy of national participatory democracy tended to diminish the value of chiefship as a stepping stone to wider power, it can be argued that it also left something of a vacuum in the Nyamwezi area, where no other major section of the population seems to have possessed the special combination of relative wealth, political experience, ambition, and formal education which chiefs and their sons quite often had in good measure. Things might have been different if the area, instead of being for so long a supplier of labour to the outside world, had had major cash crops or other forms of locally-based wealth, and if perhaps combined with this it had been a zone in which mission-based proselytisation and schooling had successfully embraced large numbers of the people, as around Kilimanjaro or in the Bukoba and Mbeya areas, for example. In such circumstances it seems likely that a more broadly based source of high quality political expertise, additional to and even possibly competitive with the major chiefs, might well have arisen and provided a continuingly vigorous supply of leadership at regional and national level.

If my preceding argument has been correct, it would appear that the special Nyamwezi combination of a chiefly polity and an economy built substantially on migrant labour – which had developed strongly in the colonial period – may have left the people in a politically weak position after the changes of the 1960s, in addition to any more direct economic costs it may have entailed for them. It is not easy, however, to measure the significance for the people of the shift involved, or to anticipate how long it will continue. Clearly it is no cause for Nyamwezi satisfaction, but it would perhaps be wrong to make too much of it in a country which is consciously striving both to counterbalance sectional loyalties in favour of a strong commitment to the nation as a whole and to extend the pool from which new leadership is drawn. The large-scale post-Independence programmes of social, political and economic development in the previously poorly but now well-represented Dodoma District – and indeed the decision to place Tanzania's new capital there – are substantial testimony to the seriousness of these policies, and it may well be that Unyamwezi has not quite so much to worry about for the future in its present level of participation in the nation's political structure as might appear at first sight. In addition, it is perhaps misleading to end this part of my discussion on even such a muted negative note and fail to say at least a little, more positively, about how the people have been able to contribute in recent years to wider Tanzanian society in other, equally important domains. In education, for example, there have been many school and university teachers from the area; and it has also produced a number of important religious dignitaries and at least two men in the highest ranks of the Tanzanian medical profession. There is thus considerable cause for satisfaction in the way that these and many other Nyamwezi are, along with their fellow Tanzanians from elsewhere, regularly applying their specialised skills in a wide variety of fields to the building of the nation whose foundations their precursors helped to lay.

The force of custom

In my Introduction I discussed the question of 'who are the Nyamwezi' and I pointed out that it involves quite complex issues of both being and becoming. As I noted then, there are well over half a million people who in certain contexts will describe themselves as Nyamwezi and who mostly recognise a close association with the Nyamwezi area and Nyamwezi language and custom. The form of this connection, however, and indeed the boundaries of the area and the form of language and custom themselves have grown and changed over relatively short periods of time; and this point is especially relevant at the present when, as we have seen, the people as a whole are in a wide variety of ways drawn more and more into the Tanzanian nation. The question which arises in this context is that of what if any meaning 'being Nyamwezi', or being Sumbwa or Sukuma for that matter, can have in the years to come for villagers in the area, and I want now to consider certain aspects of this problem.

Ethnicity is, as I have said, a delicate and sometimes a disruptive issue within nations (and, one may add, even between them), but it has been much less of a problem within Tanzania than, for instance, in Uganda. This has been largely due to a combination of, on the one hand, a firm but generally not oppressive official determination to keep the issue out of politics, and, on the other, the absence of any uncontrollably dangerous situations in the colonial legacy. People have, moreover, usually been able to combine their membership of Tanzania's cultural and linguistic sub-groups quite comfortably with a strong allegiance to the nation. In general, this has been as true of the Nyamwezi as of others. Hard-liners can occasionally be found but they appear to be genuine exceptions. For example, I have already mentioned how one Nyamwezi chief just prior to Independence appeared to be interested in a federal constitution for the country, and it seems clear that he envisaged the existence of a Nyamwezi and Sukuma section in that framework. On the other side, one can meet

The Nyamwezi Today

Nyamwezi individuals at the present time who see themselves as more or less exclusively Tanzanian and who consider matters of ethnic identity to be not even quaint or simply old-fashioned, but to be positive hindrances to the nation's socialist development.

Such viewpoints are, as I have said, exceptional and would I believe find little if any sympathy with the very large majority of the people who would much prefer not to be pressed to polarise the issues in either of these ways. They have no doubt that they are loyal Tanzanians and this is a source of substantial pride to them. At the same time, however, they derive a part of their identity from being Nyamwezi. These two sources of identity (and there are many others, of course, also) are seen as complementary to each other rather than conflicting, and this view has not so far been subjected to any serious, direct and concerted challenge. On the other hand, one cannot help noticing that a variety of processes are at work which appear likely to erode the more locally-based Nyamwezi element in the situation and people have begun to comment upon some of these. Thus a number have observed to me – and some more regretfully than others – that the spread of Swahili, which in itself is clearly of great value, may well entail the gradual diminution and possibly eventually the loss of Kinyamwezi, especially if children are not educated to take pride and pleasure in the latter language as part of their personal and national heritage. Others have noted, as I have reported earlier, that the status of locally-based law and custom is increasingly in doubt. Thus we have seen that the Primary Courts, often presided over by magistrates from elsewhere in the country, administer a sometimes quite confusing mixture of national and so-called 'customary' law, the latter being drawn officially and in ways largely beyond the people's control from various sources both outside and within Unyamwezi; and the exact powers of the more locally-based 'reconciliation tribunals' and the legality even of traditional neighbourhood courts have in recent years been matters of substantial uncertainty at the village level.

Despite these pressures, however, and notwithstanding the growing involvement of the people in the nation, an interest in local custom still remains among them. As my previous references bring out, such local custom (Kinyamwezi *shimile* or Swahili *mila* or *desturi*) is a complex and varying amalgam of behavioural rules and patterns, some of which are fairly general to a narrower or broader area of country as a whole and others, e.g. in more private fields of food taboos or marriage rules, vary between ethnic groups and even between individuals. Those which are more specific to the Nyamwezi themselves, and those which have become general to the area or a part of it, are sometimes spoken of as Nyamwezi custom (perhaps with a local area specified when this is appropriate) or they may be described simply as 'indigenous' (the Swahili term *kienyeji* is commonly used in such contexts); or again, as we have seen in Chapter 2, they may be referred to in terms of *bumamhala* ('elderhood'). Other less widespread forms may be spoken of as Sumbwa or Tusi custom, as the case may be, or even as the custom of a particular kin group, e.g. a Tusi clan.

The reasons for a popular interest in the field of custom are not necessarily those which spring immediately to mind. Unlike their function in some other places, customary differences and similarities in Unyamwezi have not been a medium for the expression of political and economic competition between different ethnic groups (with the partial historical exception of the Tusi). Moreover, as my references to 'identity' and my earlier discussion of changes in the field of kinship and marriage custom imply, the interest can by no means simply be dismissed as antiquarian. I recall being especially struck by both its strength and its conjunction with an equally strong interest in modern developments on a visit which I made in 1975 to the new village of Wame in Kahama District. As I have mentioned, this was an *ujamaa* village established under the leadership of the then District Chairman of TANU. It was visited by President Nyerere in February that year when he travelled to Shinyanga Region, and it was eventually judged officially to be the best *ujamaa* village for 1975 in the Region. During my visit there I talked with a number of the village household heads and began to ask about a range of local custom including *masumule* payments for failure to fulfil neighbourhood obligations, *mchenya* payments for eloping with an unmarried girl, and the ostracism (*bubiti*) of recalcitrant neighbours who refused to pay the *masumule* penalties imposed upon them. The interest which this discussion aroused was very clearly marked; and the Co-operative Development Officer (a man from the Moshi area) who had accompanied me on the visit was particularly impressed by the enthusiasm with which the villagers discussed such customs, which he had never heard of and which were in several cases practised in the village.

The fact that the villagers concerned were among Tanzania's pioneers of modernity, and the further fact that some of the custom in

131

question, like *mchenya*, was relatively new in the area while other forms, such as *bubiti*, were old and beginning to fall into disuse clearly render any simple argument about 'peasant conservatism' unsatisfactory as an explanation of the situation. I would suggest that custom in such contexts needs to be perceived not as something backward-looking and immutable but rather as a valuable and malleable resource which serves a variety of contemporary ends for those to whom it belongs. For many, it is a symbol and a source of their identity which has both personal and social structural implications, for it helps people to know who they are both for themselves and *vis-à-vis* each other; and from this latter point of view it is also a source of power which people who possess it may be able to use to defend and even to extend their interests. Like an adherence to a national or local language, it may perhaps at times serve as a rallying cry which leaders might exploit in order to attract and to unite their followers and perhaps increase their individual and joint power. Rather more significantly in the present context, however, it appears also to provide a way in which those who are relatively weak in material terms can try to redress the imbalance of power and prestige between themselves and those who are richer or stronger.

An incident from the late 1950s will perhaps help to bring out some aspects of this last point more clearly. It concerned a Veterinary Assistant who was in charge of the Veterinary Centre at Butumwa village where I was living at the time. He was a young and relatively well-educated Nyamwezi from another part of Kahama District, and he lived at the Centre with his wife and a young related boy who helped around the house. He also owned a motor-cycle, which he used for travel to town and to outlying areas in the course of his work and also privately, and it was his use of this vehicle which led to the occurrence of the incident in question.

The Assistant was riding along one of the roads a few miles from the Centre when he chanced to pass a group of villagers who were participating in a funeral within sight of the road. Instead of stopping in accordance with local custom in order to greet them and join for a short time in their activities, he rode on and he later claimed that he had been so busy looking out for pot-holes in the road that he had not noticed what was happening. Without delay, however, the slighted villagers sent a letter to the 'elders' of Butumwa demanding that they fine the Assistant a goat as a customary *masumule* penalty for his offence. In response to this letter, a meeting of neighbours was duly held in Butumwa and a reduced fine of beer was initially imposed, but this was raised to a goat when further pressure was applied by the complainants in a second letter. A feast was later held at which the goat was eaten and, as is customary in such circumstances, the offender participated fully in it and all the local households provided stiff porridge (*bugalli*) as a staple for the meal. None of the offended villagers was present, not because they were offended but because they were not members of Butumwa village. This again is normal practice in the area.

The incorporative quality of such procedures, and especially of the feasting, is important, but the Assistant clearly felt at the time that people had also been glad to get at him in this affair because of his relatively high status and prosperity. My own impression was that there was truth in this, though it should be added that the Assistant was in general a respectful young man, and certainly no domineering bureaucrat, and the initially reduced fine probably reflected this. Of particular interest in the present context, however, was the excited way in which a couple of our joint neighbours stressed again and again as I discussed the case with them that the Assistant had broken customary rules which he ought to have followed, and that they would 'tell him' about this.

The idea of local custom as a valuable possession which enables ordinary villagers in the Nyamwezi or other areas to assert their identity in relation to the wider world emerges fairly clearly from this case as it did also from the contrast between *serikali* and *bunamhala* that I discussed in Chapter 2. Such custom is something which is theirs and which equips them with their own special dignity and authority in situations where they are in other respects less well endowed than those with whom they may be dealing. They are poor by most objective standards – and their chances of exerting substantial influence through state structures are not really very high even in the relatively democratic Tanzanian polity. Throughout the colonial period and into Independence they have mainly been on the receiving end of power relationships, despite their positive contributions to the development of the nation, and it would be very optimistic to expect a radical change in this situation in the immediate future. To a varying extent – and of course the variation matters greatly – this has been the lot of villagers at most times and in most places, and if (as in the incident I have described) they appear occasionally to be 'small-minded', one must recall that theirs is always liable to be an uphill

133

struggle to maintain their self-respect and the respect of others in a world in which so many of the odds are weighted against them. Indeed, the notable capacity of Nyamwezi villagers (and their neighbours) for cheerful helpfulness and open hospitality to others, which I myself have experienced in full measure, is all the more remarkable in this light.

If this analysis is valid, it follows that the careless erosion of locally-based custom can easily be accompanied by an erosion of the dignity and self-esteem of those whose special possession it is, and this is clearly not desirable. Of course, the power which its 'owners' are able to wield through it is by no means equally distributed; and it is arguable that custom is not simply a weapon of defence against the outside world but that it also constitutes an instrument of domination on the inside. Thus in Unyamwezi as elsewhere it is used, and occasionally abused, by the older generation to control the young; and this must clearly be of interest to the state for whom the young are its main 'social capital', though cases of abuse – e.g. excessive fines for sexual offences – are to some extent, paradoxically, rendered more likely, as we have seen, by the presence of stranger Primary Court Magistrates and their possibly uncritical reliance on the aid of 'elders' as their source of information upon custom. An element of inter-generational opposition is, of course, intrinsic to the Nyamwezi and most other kinship systems and societies and, especially in times of social change, it is also liable to coincide to some degree with further sources of potential discord, such as differential access to education and wealth and differences of experience and attitude. The relative youth of the Veterinary Assistant whom I mentioned fits with this, and these further factors can quite easily interact in mutual exacerbation with the more general problems of the juxtaposition of youth's force and fire with age's ashen authority. For the present at least, however, such inter-generational conflict has not begun to loom large as a major point of confrontation in Nyamwezi society, since it has been mitigated by other features of the situation. Most obviously, the young themselves grow old so that the same persons are not permanently in a subordinate position, and the ability to move away from particular senior authority holders and settle elsewhere without difficulty has also helped, though it is not clear how long this will continue in the framework of new village structures. Again, the idea that the young themselves might wield authority in some contexts is not wholly alien to the people owing to their experience of young occupants of chiefship, though this was of course accompanied by very special customary credentials of legitimacy which most young did not possess.

As I have implied, time has its own partial solutions to the domination of the young by the old. This is, however, naturally less true of a further area of customary inequality which deserves mention here. The large part of my account has been concerned with Nyamwezi men and this fits well with many features of their social system. Women have never played a central role in Nyamwezi politics except for the few individuals who have succeeded to the chiefship in some areas; and economically their vital contribution to subsistence has been made mainly in the domestic context of kinship and marriage relationships, where they tend, as I have noted, to be at least formally and legally subordinate to men. I have already discussed some of the forces at work for change in this field in the chapter on kinship and marriage, and I have also mentioned how the division of labour and the special areas of female expertise which it involves give women a considerable degree of compensatory control over many of their activities despite their formal jural position. In addition, it is clear that a wife who is dissatisfied with her husband can fairly easily make life difficult for him in a variety of subtle ways; and women who find village life too burdensome can at least try to escape to towns, though male chauvinism is not confined to rural areas and not all women would like or could easily manage the rather precarious urban existence which such escape can involve.[7] The prospects for old age, for instance, may be quite daunting even for a fairly successful urban woman renegade if she remains childless and has cut herself off from her rural ties.

The case for maintaining the dignity of rural Nyamwezi men by respect for their customs is clearly weaker if it must be done at the expense of Nyamwezi women, but one hopes that this is not in fact the case. The crucial point I have tried to make here about custom is not that it must be preserved in its detail – I have indeed stressed its capacity for change – but that its role as a possession of the people needs to be acknowledged. Change which comes mainly and directly from outside, however objectively good it may appear to be, is liable to constitute a diminution of the identity of those on whom it is imposed and even, to some extent, of those on whose behalf it is imposed. Nor is such change liable to work efficiently if it is not substantially generated from within. The relative lack of success of

135

rural Women's Development Officers is pertinent here, and it should be noted that it is due not so much directly to male opposition as to a failure of such officers to rouse women's interests in their work. Clearly, pressure for change may have to come from outside on this issue, but it is to be hoped that it can be applied subtly and persuasively in ways which allow the people themselves (both men and women) to arrive at what are ultimately in considerable part their own new formulations of relationships between the sexes.

Notes

Preface
1. There are interesting discussions of this point in Gulliver's and Argyle's contributions to Gulliver (1969).

1. The people and their country
1. Some Igunga Sukuma displaced by these processes have moved as far south as Usangu in Mbeya Region where I encountered them in September 1979.
2. Roberts (1970) gives a very full account of early Nyamwezi trading activities.
3. The figures would be rather lower in some areas such as Igunga; and it may be added here that, in keeping with my earlier comments about fluctuating and uncertain boundaries, the Igunga area could arguably be considered these days to be ceasing to be part of Unyamwezi.
4. The largest herds contain as many as 2,000 head of cattle and are mainly owned by Sukuma immigrants.
5. For an interesting discussion of this and other aspects of mission activity in Unyamwezi see Nolan (1977). As this work brings out, the unusual success of the Roman Catholic mission in Ndala – to the south of Nzega – seems to have been connected with a weakness in the local chief's position at the time of its foundation and development.
6. This is recorded by Blohm (1933, pp. 193–4). His work and that of another missionary, Bösch (1930), contains a detailed if not wholly sympathetic account of many aspects of traditional Nyamwezi religion. For further references see Abrahams (1967b, pp. 77–80).
7. Audrey Richards (1956) has been central in developing an understanding of the many facets of this important aspect of ritual. See La Fontaine (1972) for an appreciation of her work in this area.

2. Political organisation
1. I am aware that my arguments in this context run rather strongly against the grain of M. E. R. Nicholson's paper (1973) on similar arrangements in Sukumaland. I can only plead that I am recording what I have seen for myself and heard from villagers and others on this subject.
2. The main task of codification and simplification was carried out before and after Independence by the late Hans Cory who was an official Government sociologist. My critical view of these efforts is not meant to detract from the value of much of Cory's more academic work on the Sukuma and other Tanzanian peoples.
3. For a full discussion of these intriguing voting patterns see the article by Hall and Lucas (1974).

Notes

3. The village

1. Cf. Speke (1864, pp. 278–9), Stanley (1890, Vol. II, pp. 397–400).
2. Cf. Malcolm (1953, pp. 47–50).
3. I have changed the names of the individuals concerned in this and the following cases for the sake of confidentiality.
4. The use of hired labour by individual farmers is disapproved because of the potential it embodies for engendering rural inequality. It appears, however, from work carried out in the Tabora area by Mr S. Rugumisa (personal communication) that labourers on tobacco farms are often relatively young and that they may try to use the work not only for cash but also as experience for subsequently starting their own farms. The fact that land is not scarce in the area is of course important here (cf. Saul and Woods, 1971, p. 110).

4. Marriage and kinship

1. Jeffreys (1951) argues that bridewealth itself should in fact properly be labelled 'child-price' in such cases. There is more to it than this, since rights in the woman are, of course, also involved in bridewealth payments but the argument is not without point. It may be noted here that I use the term bridewealth instead of the older form brideprice despite Gray's (1960) arguments. I do this partly because the Nyamwezi word for it, *nsabo*, is also their ordinary word for wealth and partly because the term brideprice, with its commercial overtones, still seems to beg too many questions about what is essentially a complex and ambiguous phenomenon. Its ambiguous nature was strongly brought out for me by the behaviour of one of my neighbours in disputes concerning two of his daughters. In the case of one who had been seduced by a distant kinsman before her marriage, he angrily exclaimed that the young man in question was 'spoiling my shop (*duka*)'. In the second case, where a married daughter committed adultery with her husband's younger brother, he (the father) not altogether reasonably accused the husband and his brother of treating her like a piece of family property, and he commented that 'I did not *sell* (*guja*) my daughter to those people. I agreed that one of them should *marry* (*tola*) her.' The contrast he drew here was equally between 'sale' and 'marriage' and between 'one' and 'many'.
2. The names of these payments, e.g. *ng'wekwe*, which refers to the man's offence in taking the girl without permission, and *kitandula kaya* (literally 'splitting the homestead'), which refers to the establishment of a new domestic group, were concerned with different facets of the establishment of the marriage. There is, not surprisingly, considerable overlap between them and named payments sometimes demanded in different forms of bridewealth marriage.
3. The amount paid tends to vary according to the wealth of the parties and the overall levels of cattle ownership in the area concerned. Considerably higher payments are thus often found in the better-stocked Sukuma areas, and I encountered figures of 40–45 head among Sukuma in Usangu.
4. For an interesting review of the literature and some of these issues see Goodenough (1970, Ch. 1) and also Leach (1955).

5. It may be noted that a number of terms for affines e.g. *bakwe* (affines), *mayu bukwi* (wife's mother) and *nkwilima* (son-in-law) are cognates of the word *kukwa*.
6. Flour mills appear also to have played a 'liberating' role for women in China. Cf. Myrdal and Kessle (1973, p. 28).
7. Bösch (1930) is particularly confused on this topic. For further examination of the theoretical issues raised by the Nyamwezi kinship system see Abrahams (1978).
8. For an ingenious discussion of some possible implications of this type of joking see de Heusch (1974).
9. Baxter has an interesting discussion of this issue in his paper 'Absence Makes the Heart Grow Fonder' (1972).

5. *The Nyamwezi in the wider world*
1. For a more detailed discussion of these regalia see Harding (1961) and Abrahams (1967a, Ch. 6).
2. There is an interesting history of Isike in Bennett (1975).
3. I am grateful to Mr J. Brush, who ran the Kahama–Geita Bus Service at that time, for information on this.
4. One of the more important of these marriage links was that between the father of the famous trader Tippu Tip and the ruling family of Unyanyembe. See Whiteley (1959).
5. For more information on these joking partnerships see Leslie (1963, pp. 35–7), Lucas (1974) and Abrahams (1967a & b). On ceremonial exchange and its functions see Mauss (1954) and Sahlins (1965).
6. Huxley (1931, Ch. X) gives a contemporary account of the early days of this well-known school.
7. Women who escape to towns ideally try to become householders and landladies and there are typically more independent women in the towns than in the rural areas (cf. Abrahams, 1961). Since Independence, women who live off their income from room-letting have at times been brought under pressure from local Party officials on the grounds that their income is 'unearned', but it seems likely that the motivation in these cases has at least occasionally been tinged with less honourable feelings of antagonism against such 'free' women.

References

Abrahams, R.G., 1961, 'Kahama Township, Western Province, Tanganyika', in *Social Change in Modern Africa*, ed. A.W. Southall. London.
    1965, 'Neighbourhood Organization: a Major Sub-system among the Northern Nyamwezi', *Africa*, 35(2): 168–86.
    1967a, *The Political Organization of Unyamwezi*. Cambridge.
    1967b, *The Peoples of Greater Unyamwezi* (Ethnographic Survey of Africa, Part XVII). International African Institute, London.
    1970, 'The Political Incorporation of non-Nyamwezi Immigrants among the Nyamwezi', in *From Tribe to Nation in Africa*, ed. R. Cohen and J.M. Middleton. Scranton, Pa.
    1977, 'Time and Village Structure in Northern Unyamwezi', *Africa*, 47(4): 372–85.
    1978, 'Aspects of the Distinction between the Sexes in the Nyamwezi and some other African Systems of Kinship and Marriage', in *Sex and Age as Principles of Social Differentiation*, ed. J.S. La Fontaine. London.
Baxter, P.T.W., 1972, 'Absence Makes the Heart Grow Fonder' in *The Allocation of Responsibility*, ed. M. Gluckman. Manchester.
Bennett, N.R., 1971, *Mirambo of Tanzania*, London.
    1975, 'Isike, *Ntemi* of Unyanyembe' in *African Dimensions*, ed. M. Karp. Boston.
Bloch, M., 1971, *Placing the Dead*. London.
Blohm, W., 1933, *Die Nyamwezi: Gesellschaft und weltbild*. Hamburg.
Bösch, F., 1930, *Les Banyamwezi, Peuple de l'Afrique Orientale*. Münster.
Fortes, M., 1958, 'Introduction' in *The Development Cycle in Domestic Groups*, ed. J. Goody. Cambridge Papers in Social Anthropology I, Cambridge.
Frankenberg, R., 1957, *Village on the Border*. London.
Goodenough, W.H., 1970, *Description and Comparison in Cultural Anthropology*. Chicago.
Gray, R.F., 1960, 'Sonjo Bride-price and the Question of African "Wife Purchase"', *American Anthropologist*, 62: 34–57.
Gulliver, P.H., 1969, *Tradition and Transition in East Africa*. London.
Hall, B. and Lucas, S., 1974, 'The Election as an Exercise in Political Communication', in *Socialism and Participation*. Election Study Committee of the University of Dar es Salaam, Dar es Salaam.
Harding, J.R., 1961, 'Conus Shell Disc Ornaments (*Vibangwa*) in Africa', *Journal of the Royal Anthropological Institute*, 91(1): 52–66.
de Heusch, L., 1974, 'The Debt of the Maternal Uncle', *Man* (N.S.), 9: 609–19.
Hill, P., 1972, *Rural Hausa*. Cambridge.
Huxley, J., 1931, *Africa View*. London.

References

Jeffreys, M.D.W., 1951, 'Lobolo is Child-price', African Studies, 10(4): 145–84.

La Fontaine, J.S., 1972, The Interpretation of Ritual. London.

Leach, E.R., 1955, 'Polyandry, Inheritance, and the Definition of Marriage', Man, 55: 182–6. (Reprinted in Leach, Rethinking Anthropology, 1961. London.)
1961, Pul Eliya. Cambridge.

Leslie, J.A.K., 1963, A Survey of Dar es Salaam. London.

Lucas, S. (ed.), 1974, Utani Relationships in Tanzania (unpublished mimeo). Dar es Salaam.

Malcolm, D.W., 1953, Sukumaland. Oxford.

Mapolu, H., 1973, 'Tradition and the Quest for Socialism', Taamuli, 4(1): 3–15. Dar es Salaam.

Mauss, M., 1954, The Gift, translated by I. Cunnison. London. First published in French, 1923.

Miller, N.N., 1968, 'The Political Survival of Traditional Leadership', Journal of Modern African Studies, 6(2): 183–98.

Myrdal, J. and Kessle, G., 1973, China: The Revolution Continued. Harmondsworth.

Nellis, J.R., 1972, A Theory of Ideology. Oxford.

Nicholson, M.E.R., 1973, 'Change Without Conflict: a Case Study of Legal Change in Tanzania', Law and Society Review, Summer 1973: 747–66.

Nolan, F.P., 1977, Christianity in Unyamwezi (Ph.D. Dissertation, University of Cambridge).

Nyerere, J.K., 1967a, Socialism and Rural Development. Dar es Salaam.
1967b, The Arusha Declaration. Dar es Salaam.
(1967a and b are reprinted in J.K. Nyerere, Freedom and Socialism. London, 1968.)
1973, Report to the TANU Conference September 1973. Dar es Salaam.

Prime Minister's Office, Tanzania, 1975, Sheria ya Kuandikisha Vijiji na Vijiji vya Ujamaa (booklet on Villages & Ujamaa Villages Act). Dodoma.

Richards, A.I., 1956, Chisungu: A Girl's Initiation Ceremony Among the Bemba. London.

Roberts, A., 1970, 'Nyamwezi Trade' in Pre-Colonial African Trade, ed. R. Gray and D. Birmingham. London.

Sahlins, M., 1965, 'On the Sociology of Primitive Exchange', in The Relevance of Models in Social Anthropology, ed. M. Banton. A.S.A. Monographs I. London.

Saul, J.S., and Woods, R., 1971, 'African Peasantries', in Peasants and Peasant Societies, ed. T. Shanin. Harmondsworth.

Southall, A.W., 1970, 'The Illusion of Tribe', Journal of Asian and African Studies, 5: 28–50.

Speke, J.H., 1864, What Led to the Discovery of the Source of the Nile. London.

Stanley, H.M., 1890, In Darkest Africa, London.

Swantz, M-L., 1970, Ritual and Symbol in Traditional Zaramu Society. Uppsala.

References

Tanzania. *Report on the 1967 Census*. Vol. V: Methodology. Central Statistical Bureau, Dar es Salaam.

UNESCO. 1968, 'Age Data in African Censuses and Surveys', E/CN14/CPH/ 13.

Whiteley, W.H. (ed.), 1959, *Maisha ya Hamed bin Muhammed el Mujerbi yaani Tippu Tip* (autobiography of Tippu Tip). *Journal of East African Swahili Committee*, 28–9 (1958–9), Supplement.

Index

Index

Kisuke village, 67, 83, 84, 86, 89
Konongo, 11

labour migration, 10–11, 16, 39, 68, 125, 128
Leach, E. R., 72, 138
Leslie, J. A. K., 139
Lucas, S., 139
Lugusha, N., 126

magistrates, 34, 36, 40ff, 130, 134
Malcolm, D. W., 138
Mapolu, H., 71
marriage, 59, 63–4, 69
  functions of, 105–9
  incidence of, 101–5
  see also bridewealth, children (rights over), divorce, domestic groups, polygyny, women (status of)
Mauss, M., 139
Miller, N. N., 37
Mirambo, 10, 28
Myrdal, J. and Kessle, G., 139

Nellis, J. R., 2
Nicholson, M. E. R., 137
Nolan, F. P., 137
Nyamwezi, significance of name, 2–5
Nyamwezi society
  open nature of, vii, x, 4, 5, 6, 12, 20, 22, 39, 122

Parliament (Bunge), 49
  elections to, 49, 81
politics, Chapter 2 passim
  participation in, 39–53
  see also CCM, Parliament, TANU
polygyny, 63–4, 81, 89, 102, 104, 112, 119
population
  Tanzanian, 1
  Nyamwezi, 3
  Tabora Town, 14
  mixed nature of, x, 12, 15, 91
  mobility of, 8, 11–12, 13, 21, 59–70, 91

Reconciliation Tribunals
  (mabaraza ya usuluhishi), 44, 130
Region (Mkoa), 35
religion, ix, 19–25, 128
Richards, A. I., 137

Roberts, A., 137
Rugumisa, S., 138

Sahlins, M., 71, 139
Saul, J. and Woods, R., 138
Sazia, L., 127
shops, 14–15
Southall, A. W., x
Speke, J. H., 138
spirit possession, 21–2
Stanley, H. M., 138
Sukuma, 3, 8, 131
Sumbwa, 12, 131
Swahili, ix, 1, 14, 16–17, 36, 40, 44, 130
Swantz, M-L., 67

TANU, 1, 2, 26, 28, 30, 31, 34, 36, 43, 47, 48, 49, 50–2, 70, 74, 119, 123, 127
  see also CCM
Tabora School, 31, 125
ten-house cells (mashina), 34, 76
trade, 10–11, 16, 27, 123
Tusi, 3, 5, 12, 13, 131

ujamaa, 2, 45, 54–5, 72, 76, 82–9, 110, 120–1
Ulowa I Village, 84–5, 89
urban society, contrast with rural, 14, 16, 45–6, 52–3
utani (joking partnerships), 3, 123, 124–5

villages, 34, 40, 45, 50–2, Chapter 3, 96, 123, 131
  age structure in, 60–70
  customary co-operation in, 70–5, 131–2
  form of post-1974, 74, 75–82, 82–9, 96, 123, 131
  form of pre-1974, 56–70
  see also ujamaa, Village Registration Act, villagisation
Village Managers, 51
Village Registration Act, 50, 55, 75, 77
villagisation, 45, 49, 55, 75, 80–1, 82–3, 89
Vumilia village, 84

Wame village, 84, 85, 89, 131
war
  19th Century, 10, 123
  with Uganda, 1, 13–14, 50, 79
Ward (Kata), 33, 36, 51

144